Portrait of Fr Joseph Dunn

Census of the Catholic Congregation of Preston 1810 and 1820

by

Rev. Joseph Dunn

Transcribed by Margaret Purcell

Ancestral Data Publications

First Published in 1993 by:

Ancestral Data Publications
11 Waller Avenue
Blackpool
Lancashire FY2 9EL

© Sanctuary Books 1993

British Library Cataloguing-in-Publication Data
A catalogue record for this book is
available from the British Library

ISBN 1-898487-00-6

Printed in Great Britain by:

T Snape & Company Ltd
Bolton's Court
Preston, Lancashire, PR1 3TY

Contents

Introduction		1
Notes and Acknowledgments		3
Abbreviations used in listings		4
1810 Census Listings		5
Example of 1810 entries		76
1820 Census Listings		77
Example of 1820 entries		181
Explanatory Comments		183
List of Preston Streets		184
Portrait of Fr Joseph Dunn		Opposite Title Page
Old photograph of St Wilfrid's Church		Opposite Page 1

Old photograph of St Wilfrid's Church

Introduction

The census of 1810 and that of 1820 are contained in a single volume. On its title page, someone (the binder?) has written in pencil "Mr Dunn's Book". "Mr Dunn" was the name used by the priest in charge of the Catholic Mission of Preston from 1783 until his death, in 1827, at the age of eighty-one.

Whether it was his real name, or an alias, is not known. The earliest authorities, Peter Whittle, the Liverpool Mercury of 1829, Dr George Oliver and Brother Henry Foley, SJ., all say that his real name was Hart, and the Necrology of the English Province of the Society of Jesus agrees. Joseph Gillow, relying on the entry for Fr Dunn's brother, Fr William Dunn, in the register of St Gregory's, Paris, says that his real name was Earpe and that his father was perhaps steward to the Maire or Lawson families. Neither Earpe nor Hart appear in the Returns of Papists in Catterick in 1767. Sir Henry Lawson had a coachman surnamed Yarp, which is perhaps how Earpe was pronounced, and Ann Maire of Durham, in her Will dated December 1746, mentions a godson "Joseph Earp". This could be the Reverend Joseph Dunn (Earpe or Hart), born Catterick on 19 March 1746, who entered the Society of Jesus in 1764. Ordained priest in 1771, he was teaching in the school at Bruges when the Society of Jesus was suppressed by Pope Clement XIV in 1773.

When that school was closed, masters and pupils repaired to Liège Academy. Three of these masters, Fr Nicholas Sewall, Fr Joseph Dunn and Fr Richard Morgan, were later to work in Preston. Fr Sewall was the first. He arrived in Preston in 1774, in which year Fr Dunn went as chaplain to the Clavering family at Callaly Castle, near Whittingham, Northumberland. From there, he was summoned to assist Fr Sewall who was finding the rapidly increasing demands of the Preston Mission too much for one priest. He arrived on 1 May 1776. Later, in 1814, he was to state that there were fewer than five hundred Catholics in Preston when he first came. This figure, in view of other evidence, must be taken to refer to attendance at Sunday Mass. The 1767 Returns of Papists for the Diocese of Chester list 1043 Catholics living in Preston, and Fr Francis Blundell, SJ., in a letter of 2 February 1774 puts the number of Catholics in Preston at 1100.

In 1783, Fr Sewall was replaced by Fr Richard Morgan and Fr Dunn took charge. The first Catholic Relief Act and the rapid increase in the urban population, resulting from the Industrial Revolution, offered new challenges and opportunities. Fr Dunn was quick to respond. His first care was to open a Sunday School to teach children of the poor to read and to practice their religion. It was a split-site school. The girls were taught in the lower part of the house of the school mistress, Mary Walmesley; the boys in a barn open and cold, at the top of Roast Beef Yard. It began in 1787 with fewer than a hundred pupils. In 1792, besides building the church of St Wilfrid's and a clergy house, Fr Dunn moved the schools to two purpose built rooms at the upper end of Mount Street. By 1814, numbers had grown to 302 and a new school, still in use, was built in Fox Street. Two years later, a Catholic cemetery, with its own mortuary chapel, was opened in St Wilfrid's Street near the school. As Dr Oliver justly observes "In his declining years, Mr Dunn, had the consolation of witnessing thr Missionary establishment of Preston ranking among the most respectable and best organised of any in the Kingdom".

Fr Dunn was in his sixty-fifth year when he took the census of 1810 which for the most part is written in a somewhat shaky hand not unlike his own. The census of 1820 appears to have been recorded by a very much younger scribe; the handwriting being almost copperplate. The information provided by these two censuses will be of use and interest, not only to those trying to trace their Prestonian ancestors, but to all working in the fields of local, ecclesiastical or social history, giving as they do such detailed information about an urban congregation at the height of the Industrial Revolution. For Catholics baptised or married in Preston between 1803 and 1812, they provide a unique source of information, since registers for that period have been missing for more than one hundred years.

With reference, doubtless, to the part he played in the establishment of the Preston Gas Company, of the House of Recovery and of the Catholic circulating library, Fr Dunn's memorial tablet in St Wilfrid's church says of him that "he efficiently forwarded undertakings of public utility", and the Liverpool Mercury of 27 March 1829 remarks "the well being of Society seemed to be the grand object he pursued through a long, laborious, pious and most meritorious life". Fr Denis Blackledge SJ. in permitting and Miss Margaret Purcell in initiating and bringing to its conclusion the publication of this work, have earned the blessing of Fr Dunn by making available to the present generation this his latest contribution to public utility.

Fr Francis Keegan SJ.

Notes and Acknowledgments

Although a literal transcription of Fr Joseph Dunn's census of his Preston congregation was intended, some adjustments were needed for publication.

The 1810 census differs from 1820 in that letters indicating likely relationships were given for some families, Christian names and street names were abbreviated, and no house numbers were shown. Relationships and ages, where recorded, have been printed in separate columns, whereas originally, they were listed in one column. In general, relationships will be obvious, ie. Father (F), Mother (M), Son (S) and Daughter (D). To avoid confusion, other letters have been allocated to the less frequently occurring relationships, eg. Grandson/Granddaughter (GS/GD), Sister (Si). (W) had been shown for Wife, Widow or Widower. As it has been possible to differentiate between these conditions, the following letters have been adopted: Wife (Wf), Widow (Wd) or Widower (Wr). Husband is now (Hu). In the 1820 census, the word "Street" was omitted from many of the addresses.

Surnames were mostly repeated line by line in 1810. A blank may be taken to be a repeat of the surname immediately above, as in the 1820 census. For convenience, the number of lines published per page has been standardised, although the original records vary in number with each page. Surnames on the first line of each page have now been enclosed in square brackets when assumed from the previous page.

Ages were generally shown in years, with some recorded in months or weeks. Any age given as a fraction of a year has been converted to months, and a comment added separately. An "x" or "+" occurs against many names in the earlier census. Their meaning is not known, but could indicate an adult or older child.

Included with a few entries in 1810 were the letters "O" or "P". It has not been possible to make a reasonable assumption as to their meaning, and so, these letters have been omitted.

Where Fr Dunn included additional information, his remarks are recorded in inverted commas in the Comments listed after the 1820 census. Any other difficulty in transcription has been listed here also.

A Directory of Preston streets in 1821, taken from Whittle's "Account of the Borough of Preston" has been added to help interpret the shortened form of street names. The history of the Catholic Congregation of Preston is told in the book "Through Twenty Preston Guilds - The Catholic Congregation of St Wilfrid's" by Leo Warren, published in 1993 to mark the 200th anniversary of the opening of the new chapel of St Wilfrid's on 4 June 1793.

My thanks are due to Fr D Blackledge SJ, Fr B Parkin SJ, and Fr F Keegan SJ of St Wilfrid's, for allowing me to transcribe Fr Dunn's census and for their help whilst the work was in progress. Also, I would like to thank Mr D Galvin for his advice and assistance during preparation. Finally, I must place on record a debt of gratitude to those friends of Catholic Family and Local History, who contributed towards the cost of this publication.

Margaret Purcell

D	Daughter		m	month
F	Father		w	week
GD	Granddaughter			
GF	Grandfather			
GM	Grandmother			
GS	Grandson			
Hu	Husband			
Inf	Infant			
M	Mother			
S	Son			
Si	Sister			
St	Stepmother			
Sv	Servant			
Wd	Widow			
Wf	Wife			
Wr	Widower			

a) Relationship Column   b) Age Column

Abbreviations used in Tables

1810 Census   Catholic Congregation of Preston

Surname	Forename(s)	Rel	Age	Address	Comm
Arrowsmith	Ellen			Cpl St	
Ainsworth	John			W Sq	
Atherton	Richard			do	
Atkinson	Alice	M		Fishg -	
Atkinson	Mary	D	25		
Atkinson	Jas	S			
Anderson	Nancy	M			
Anderson	Wm	S	6		
Anderson	Richd		3		
Appleton	Mary			Sprig	
Abbot	Will.			Cnl St	
Adamson	John	F			
Adamson	Agnes	M			
Adamson	Richd.	S	13		
Adamson	Jane		10		
Adamson	Mary		7		
Adamson	Eliz		4		
Adamson	John		1		
Adams	Betty			Stch h	
Anderson	Hannah	M		Bck L	
Anderson	Wm	S	7		
Anderson	Edw	S	5		
Anderson	Robt		1		
Appleton	Jos	F		Nth St	
Appleton	Helen	M			
Appleton	Tho		10		
Appleton	Ann		9		
Appleton	Cath		7		
Appleton	John		5		
Appleton	James		3		
Appleton	Clare		1		
Astly	Jas	F		Ty B St	
Astly	Marg	M			
Astly	Marg	D	1		
Abbot	John	F		Spt M	
Abbot	Sarah	M			
Abbot	John	S	17+		
Abbot	Marg	D	14+		
Abbot	Jane	D	12		
Abbot	Matty	D	4		
Arrowsmith	Betty			Ch St	
Alston	Thos			Brg St	
Ascroft	Widdow			Fr g B	
Arkwright	John	F		Fr g Ch	
Arkwright	Eliz	M			
Arkwright	Rich	S	9		
Arkwright	Will		5		
Arkwright	Henry		3		
Ainsworth	Betty		25	Wd St	
Ainsworth	Mary		2		

1810 Census   Catholic Congregation of Preston

Surname	Forename(s)	Rel	Age	Address	Comm
Armriding	Jas	F		Hldn Sq	
Armriding	Mary	M			
Armriding	Betty		23		
Armriding	Sylvester		19		
Armriding	Agnes		14		
Answorth	Margarat				
Artholony	Margt				
Ainsworth	John	Sv			1
Atherton	Richard	Sv			1
Abraham	Mary	M		Friergate	
	William				
	Betty				
Alexander	William	F		Friergate	2
	Ann	M			
	Alice				
	William				
	Margaret		6		
	Jane		4		
Ackers	Peter	F			
	Agnes	M			
	Thomas				
	Catherine				
Annolde	Mark				
Astley	Edwd			Taylors Gardens	
Astley	John		22		
Astley	William		20		
Astley	Winifred		16		
Astley	Edwd		6		
Adrington	Ann		46		
Adrington	William		15		
Adrington	Fanny		11		
Adrington	Cathe		2		
Adrington	Joseph		4		
Anderson	Hannah	M		Back Lane	
	William		7		
	Edward		5		
	Robert		1		
Adams	Betty			Starchhouse	
Appleton	Joseph	F		Vicar St	
	Ellin	M			
	Thos		10		
	Ann		9		
	Catherine		7		
	John		5		
	James		3		
	Clare		1		
Arclay	Ellin		x		
Ascroft	Ann	Sv	17x	Chirch St	
Arrowsmith	Betty	Sv	24x		
Armriding	Jane	Wd			

6

1810 Census — Catholic Congregation of Preston

Surname	Forename(s)	Rel	Age	Address	Comm
Armriding	James		3		
Armriding	Henry		9m		3
Abram	William			Leeming St	
Atkinson	Thos	F		Leeming St	
Atkinson	Mary	M			
Atkinson	Mary		6		
Atkinson	Thos		4		
Ashton	James	F			
Ashton	Betty	M			
Ashton	Catherine		7		
Ashton	Ellen		5		
Ashton	Betty		1		
Ackers	Henry	F			
Ackers	Betty	M			
Ackers	Thos		14w		
Ackers	William	F			
Ackers	Betty	M			
Ackers	Mary		10		
Ackers	Ann		8		
Ashton	John	F		Cnl St	
Ashton	Winney	M			
Ashton	Winney		32		
Ashton	James		25		
Ashton	John		12		
Apleton	William				
Apleton	Ellen				
Armstrong	Elizth			Cr St	
Anderton	Rich	F			
Anderton	Betty	M			
Anderton	Elizth		19		
Anderton	Jane		16		
Adkinson	John	F			
Adkinson	Jane	M			
Adkinson	James		1		
Billington	Mary	Sv		Frg	
Brewer	Ellen	M		Cpl St	
Brewer	Martha		15		
Brewer	Mary		14		
Brewer	Eliz		12		
Brewer	Susan		9		
Barton	Wm			Fshg-	
Blanchard	Jas	F			
Blanchard	Ann	M			
Blanchard	John	S	2		
Bryars	Mary				
Bamber	Hugh	F			
Bamber	Helen	M			
Bamber	Mary		5		
Bamber	John		3		
Bamber	Jas		1		

1810 Census   Catholic Congregation of Preston

Surname	Forename(s)	Rel	Age	Address	Comm
Barrow	John			Evr G	
Barrow	Sar				
Berry	Rob			Hgh St	
Berry	Mary				
Barker	Marg				
Butler	Betty	M			
Butler	Mary		+		
Butler	Jas		+		
Butler	Ann		12		
Butler	Betty		10		
Butler	Jos		8		
Butler	Rebec		5		
Bamber	John			Wkr St	
Bamber	Ann				
Ball	Mary		18	Cnl St	
Bickerstaff	Jane	M		Wkr St	
Bickerstaff	James		3		
Bickerstaff	George		1		
Bell	Hugh	F		Cnl St	
Bell	Betty	M			
Bell	Betty	D	+		
Bell	Ellen		13		
Bell	John		8		
Bell	J		1		
Bamber	Edw	F			
Bamber	Mary	M			
Bamber	Betty	D	5		
Billsbro	Tho	F			
Billsbury	Alice	M			
Billsborough	Henry		+		
Billsbro	Tho		13		
Billsbro	Betty		10		
Billsbro	Rich		7		
Billsbury	Ann		4		
Bland	Mary	M			
Bland	Jos		2		
Barns	Alice	M			
Barns	Betty		7		
Barns	Marg		1		
Barker	Jas	F		Stch H	
Barker	Marg	M			
Barker	Thos		+		
Barker	Mary		11		
Barker	Marg		1		
Barker	John		5	St	
Banks	Richd	F		Bck L	
Banks	Betty	M			
Banks	Nancy		10		
Banks	Marg		9		
Banks	Mary		8		

1810 Census   Catholic Congregation of Preston

Surname	Forename(s)	Rel	Age	Address	Comm
Barns	Wm	F		Nth St	
Barns	Nancy	M			
Barns	Rich		18		
Barns	Betty		16		
Barns	Isab		13		
Barns	Alice		11		
Barns	Mary		8		
Barns	Margt		7		
Blackburn	Tho	F			
Blackburn	Mary	M			
Blackburn	Mary		2		
Brindle	Ellen	M		Ty B St	
Brindle	Will		+		
Brindle	Betty		+		
Brindle	Jane		+		
Brindle	Charles		+		
Blackburn	James	F		Spt M	
Blackburn	Betty	M			
Blackburn	Wm		14		
Blackburn	Ric		9		
Blackburn	Cath		6		
Blackburn	Betty	M			
Blackburn	Will		11		
Brown	Marg		20		
Brown	Betty		18		
Brown	Nancy		16		
Brown	Thos		14		
Brown	James		9		
Blacksondale	Agnes	M			
Blacksondale	Wm		13		
Blacksondale	Mary		4		
Baxendale	John		2		
Bilsboro	Jas	F			
Bilsboro	Alice	M			
Billsboro	John		14		
Billsboro	Ellen		11		
Billsboro	Thos		9		
Billsboro	Rich		6		
Billsboro	Jane		4		
Billsboro	Henry		2		
Belshaw	Esther	M		Ch St	
Belshaw	Wm		8		
Bateson	Jas	F		Moor	
Bateson	Marg	M			
Bateson	Alice		+		
Bateson	Ellen		+		
Bateson	Jas		14		
Bateson	Betty		+		
Bateson	Mary		10		
Blackburn	Ellen			Ch St	

1810 Census   Catholic Congregation of Preston

Surname	Forename(s)	Rel	Age	Address	Comm
Ball	John	F		O H C	
Ball	Mary	M			
Ball	-		1		
Brindle	Rachel			Fishw	
Barton	Hugh			Htly S	
Barton	Eliz	M			
Barton	Eliz		5		
Barton	Robt		4		
Baines	Marg		18		
Belshaw	John			Frig	
Belshaw	Ann	M			
Belshaw	Eliz		15		
Belshaw	Wm		12		
Blackburn	Jas	Hu			
Blackburn	-	W			
Billington	John	F		Brg St	
Billington	Mary	M			
Billington	James		15		
Billington	John	GS	7		
Bullen	Wid			Heatly St	
Bullen	John		47		
Barns	Jas		40		
Barns	Jane				
Banks	Wm	F		Brg S	
Banks	Dol	M			
Banks	Francis		13		
Banks	Eliz		12		
Banks	Lucy		6		
Banks	Mary		1		
Banks	Thos	F			
Banks	Martha				
Banks	John		21		
Banks	Ellen		9		
Bradly	Thos	F		Frg Crrs	
Bradly	Mary	M			
Bradly	Thos	S	10		
Bradly	John		7		
Bradly	Eliz		6		
Bradly	Edw		3		
Bradly	Rich		1		
Brown	John	F		Frg	
Brown	Ann	M			
Brown	Mary	D	4		
Brown	Edw		3		
Brown	Tho		1		
Banks	Wm	F			
Banks	Thos		25		
Banks	Jos		19		
Banks	Marg		23		
Banks	Jos	GS	6		

1810 Census   Catholic Congregation of Preston

Surname	Forename(s)	Rel	Age	Address	Comra
Banks	Wid				
Banks	Peter	S	12		
Banks	Thos	F			
Banks	Ann	M			
Banks	Thos	S	2m		
Banks	Jos		19		
Banks	Mary		8		
Barton	Tho	F			
Barton	Hugh		5		
Blackburn	Wid				
Blackburn	Tho		10		
Blackburn	Greg		7		
Blackburn	Vincent		4		
Blackburn	Alice		1		
Bains	Mary Ann				
Bains	Jane		14		
Bains	Mary		12		
Bains	Thos Ant		11		
Blundell	Ann	Sv	34	Ld St	
Banks	Mary			Dle S	
Banks	Thos	F			
Banks	Mary	M			
Banks	Jas		21		
Banks	John		19		
Banks	Ann		16		
Banks	Ellen		15		
Banks	Heny		13		
Banks	Mary		11		
Banks	Hah		9		
Banks	Alice		7		
Brady	Danl			Hldn Sq	
Brady	Rose				
Banks	Mary			Stnly St	
Banks	Betty		21		
Banks	John		12		
Banks	Mary		4		
Billington	Jas	F		Cnl St	
Billington	Cath	M			
Billington	Wm		9		
Billington	Bella		7		
Billington	John		4		
Bickerstaff	John	F			
Bickerstaff	Edw		5		
Bickerstaff	Robt		3		
Bamber	Betty		+		
Bamber	Marg		+		
Bamber	Thos		+		
Barton	John	F			
Barton	Alice	M			
Barton	Lewis		4		

1810 Census   Catholic Congregation of Preston

Surname	Forename(s)	Rel	Age	Address	Comm
Barton	Jos		2		
Barton	Ann		1		
Butler	Robt	F		Sing r	
Butler	Alice	M			
Butler	Betty		1		
Bamber	Jenny				
Brown	Margery	M			
Brown	Betty		18		
Brown	Mathew		17		
Brown	Mary		13		
Brown	John		12		
Brown	Rich		8		
Brown	Jas		3		
Banks	Thos	F			
Banks	Mary	M			
Banks	Phil		3		
Banks	Betty		5		
Banks	Thos				
Banks	Betty				
Banks	Bella		5		
Banks	Betty		4		
Banks	Charles		2		
Banks	John		1		
Boardly	Betty				
Banks	Wm	F		Con St	
Banks	Nancy	M			
Banks	Joseph		1		
Billington	Ellen			Mk St	
Banks	Jos		18		
Baxter	Mary		13+		
Billington	Jenny				
Billington	Jas				
Banks	Phil	F			
Banks	Marg	M			
Banks	Mary	D	+		
Banks	Marg	D	+		
Banks	Phil		12		
Ball	Wm	F			
Ball	Ellen	M			
Ball	John	S	13		
Ball	Eliz	D	10		
Ball	Alice	D	8		
Bamber	Wm			Charlotte St	
Bamber	Nancy				
Bamber	Agnes		16		
Bamber	Oswald		14		
Bamber	Cath		12		
Bamber	Betty		10		
Bamber	Alice		5		
Bamber	Mary		1		

1810 Census — Catholic Congregation of Preston

Surname	Forename(s)	Rel	Age	Address	Comm
Bamber	Ann		1		
Baldwin	Wm				
Baldwin	Agn				
Baldwin	Dolly				
Barnes	Mary		60		
Baldwin	Betty		1		
Baldwin	Mary		2		
Brindle	Wm			Kg St	
Barker	Jas	F			
Barker	Rachel	M			
Barker	Mary		18		
Barker	Rachel		16		
Barker	Richd		14		
Blundell	John	F		Cch St	
Blundell	Ann	M			
Blundell	James		23		
Blundell	Margaret		15		
Barret	Margaret	M			
Barret	Anne		8		
Barton	William				
Bradly	William	F		Lby St	
Bradley	Mary Rebecka	M			
Bradley	Elizabeth		12		
Brand	John	F		Ch St	
Brand	Hannah	M			
Brand	John		11		
Brand	Frances Mary		3		
Bamber	Elling				
Brown	Margaret				
Brown	Edward				
Brown	Ann				
Brown	John	F			
	Alice	M			
	James		7		
	Mary		1		
Baines	James				
	Ann				
Brindle	Ellin	Wd		Walton St	
Brindle	Martha		7		
Barlow	Moses	Sv	16		
Booth	Margret	M		Leeming St	
Booth	Rossamond				
Booth	John				
Berry	Mary				
Brindle	Alice				
Barker	Dorothy	M			
Barker	James				
Bains	John		12	Queen St	
Bains	Edwd	F			
Bains	Mary	M			

1810 Census   Catholic Congregation of Preston

Surname	Forename(s)	Rel	Age	Address	Comm
Bains	Mary		18		
Bains	John		15		
Bains	Alice		13		
Bains	Ann		11		
Bains	Edmund		9		
Bains	Ellen		7		
Bains	Margret		1		
Bains	Hannah				
Billington	Jane	M			
Billington	Betty				
Billington	Mary		9		
Billington	Betty		7		
Bonney	James	F			
Bonney	Ann	M			
Bonney	Margret		15		
Bonney	Ann		10		
Barton	Hugh	F		Heatley St	
Barton	Elizabeth	M			
Barton	Elizth		5		
Barton	Robt		4		
Bains	Margret		18		
Balshaw	John	F		Friergate	
Balshaw	Ann	M			
Balshaw	Elizth		15		
Balshaw	William		12		
Blackburn	James				
Blackburn	Mrs				
Billington	John	F		Bridget St	
Billington	Mary	M			
Billington	James		15		
Billington	John	GS	7		
Bulon	Wm			Heatley St	
Bulon	John		47		
Barns	James		40		
Barns	Jane				
Banks	William			Bridget St	
Banks	Dolly	M			
Banks	Frances		19		
Banks	Elizth		12		
Banks	Lucy		6		
Banks	Nancy		1		
Banks	Thos	F			
Banks	Martha	M			
Banks	John		21		
Banks	Ellen		19		
Banks	W			Friergate	
Banks	Peeter		12		
Banks	Thos	F			
Banks	Ann	M			
Banks	Thos		27		

1810 Census   Catholic Congregation of Preston

Surname	Forename(s)	Rel	Age	Address	Comm
Banks	Joseph		19		
Banks	Mary		8		
Barton	Thos	F			
Barton	Isabella	M			
Barton	Hugh		5		
Blackburn	W				
Blackburn	Thos		10		
Blackburn	Gregory		7		
Blackburn	Vincent		4		
Blackburn	Alice		1		
Barns	Ann Mary				
Barns	Jane		14		
Barns	Mary		12		
Barns	Thos Antony		12		
Blacow	Mr			Frierg	
Bleasdail	Betty			Brige St	
Billington	Ann				
Birkit	James				
Billington	Thos		21		
Biting	Widow			Heatly St	
Chorley	James			Evr G	
Cottam	John	F		Hgh St	
Cottam	Mary	M			
Cottam	Barthol		+		
Cottam	Ellen		+		
Cottam	Ellis		+		
Cottam	Bella		12		
Cottam	Ann		10		
Cottam	Margt		2		
Cottam	John Jnr	F			
Cottam	Ann	M			
Cottam	Mary Ann	D	1		
Crumbleholm	Ann	M			
Crumbleholm	Tho		12		
Crumbleholm	John				
Crumbleholm	Mary				
Crumbleholm	Lewis				
Chew	Dorothy				
Caton	Wm			Hgh St.Wlker St	
Caton	Jane	M			
Caton	Wm	S	+		
Caton	Susan		+		
Caton	Robt		+		
Caton	Bella		14		
Catteral	Ann	M			
Catteral	James	S	6		
Caddy	Johnoth	F			
Caddy	Mary	M			
Caddy	John		6		
Caddy	Ann		4		

1810 Census   Catholic Congregation of Preston

Surname	Forename(s)	Rel	Age	Address	Comm
Caddy	Betty		1		
Cock	Heny	F			
Cock	Alice	M			
Cook	Jos	S	+		
Crosly	Jane			Wlk S	
Collins	Doroth				
Collier	Alice			Cnl St	
Cragg	Jane				
Counsel	Mary				
Cook	Bella				
Chew	John	F		Moor L	
Chew	Mary	M			
Chew	John		14		
Chew	Jos		10		
Catteral	John	F		Moor L	
Catteral	Ann	M			
Catteral	Thos		9		
Crook	Ann			Cpl St	
Champion	Anne	M		Fshg	
Champion	Betty	D			
Champion	Cath	D			
Curry	John	F			
Curry	Jane	M			
Curry	Wm	S	18		
Curry	John	S	8		
Curry	Charles		4		
Crumbleholm	Math			Spit M	
Crumbleholm	Betty				
Crumbleholm	Ellen		+		
Crumbleholm	John		8		
Crumbleholm	Tho		6		
Crumbleholm	Winif		4		
Crumbleholm	Rich		1		
Cowell	Wm	F		Fshw	
Cowel	Hel		+		
Cowel	John	S	+		
Cowel	Isab	D	+		
Cowel	Wm	S	+		
Cowel	Alice		13		
Cuerden	Ann	Sv		Ld St	
Chadwick	Margt	M			
Chadwick	Margt	D	10		
Chadwick	Frank		8		
Chadwick	John				
Chadwick	Heny				
Chadwick	Mary				
Chew	Jos	F		Shamb	
Chew	Ann	M			
Carr	Ann	M			
Carr	Dor		+		

1810 Census — Catholic Congregation of Preston

Surname	Forename(s)	Rel	Age	Address	Comm
Carr	Marg		+		
Carr	Rich		10		
Clayton	Wm				
Cuerden	Jas		17+		
Cardwell	Mrs				
Cuerden	Marg				
Cuerden	Mary				
Cuerden	Rebec				
Cooper	Alice				
Cottam	Th			Kg St	
Cottam	Jane				
Cottam	Ann		12		
Cottam	-		4		
Caton	Robt	F		Parke l	
Caton	Betty	M			
Caton	Jas		5		
Caton	Betty		1		
Caton	Wm		3		
Calvert	Edw			Charlotte St	
Calvert	Mary				
Caupe	John	F		Kg St	
Caupe	Mary	M			
Caupe	John	S	46		
Corbishly	John			Frg	
Clayton	James	F		Rose St	
Clayton	Margaret	M			
Clayton	John		Inf		
Cockerell	Jane		74		
Cockerell	Nancy		45		
Cockerell	Mary		37		
Chew	Mary			School St	
Catterall	Paul	F		Church St	
Catterall	Mrs	M			
Cottam	Jane		+	Starch hous	
Cuerden	Matthew		+	Back lane	
Cuerden	Sarah		+		
Cuerden	Mary		7		
Cuerden	William		5		4
Chorley	Ellen	M		near Vicar St	
Chorley	Mary		9		
Curry	William	F		Vic St	
Curry	William		7		
Curry	James		1		
Carr	John	F		Mill St	
Carr	Susannah	M	46		
Carr	Margaret		15		
Carr	John		12		
Carr	Thomas		5		
Carry	Henry		3		
Carr	Alice		1		

1810 Census   Catholic Congregation of Preston

Surname	Forename(s)	Rel	Age	Address	Comm
Connel	Miles			Feeble St	
Cornthwaite	Andrew	F		Mill St	
Cornthwaite	Betty	M			
Cornthwaite	James		16		
Cornthwaite	Jane		11		
Cook	Sarah			Tythe Barn	
Caton	Elling	M		Ch St	
	Mary				
Crook	Thos	F		Ribbleton Lane	
	Mary	M			
	Margarat		1		
Crook	Wm	F			
	Betty	M			
	Thomas				
	Edward				
	John				
	Richard				
	Alexander				
	William		11		
	Nancy		9		
	Jane		7		
	Sylvaster		5		
	Benedict Joseph		4		
Carter	Thomas	F		Chch St	
	Mary	M			
	Robert		12		
	Andrew		10		
	John		8		
	Ann		6		
Cannigan	John			Ribbleton lane	
Collison	Edward	F		Moor	
	Catherine	M			
	John		8		
	Christopher		5		
	Nancy		2		
Coin	Sarah	M		Ribbletn lane	
	William		7		
	Richard		1		
Carter	Dorothy				
Clarkson	Isabella				
Crook	Elizabeth		22	Blk H Yd	
Crow	Thomas				
Cait	Joseph	F			
	Mary	M			
	Mary		8		
	James		6		
	Elling		4		
	Ann		2		
Crombleholme	David	F			
	Elling	M			

18

1810 Census   Catholic Congregation of Preston

Surname	Forename(s)	Rel	Age	Address	Comm
[Crombleholme]	Betty				
	Margaret				
	Thomas				
	James				
	Ann				
Cooper	Henry				
Cardwell	Alice		62	Walton St	
Cook	Ann				
Campbell	Owen			Leeming St	
Chambers	Mary				
Coupe	James				
Coupe	Alice				
Carter	James				
Carter	Betty				
Cannon	Barnaby Mr	F		York St	
Cannon	Charles Mr		10		
Cannon	James Mr		6		
Cannon	John Mr		1		
Cranshaw	Peter	F			
Cranshaw	Betty	M			
Cranshaw	Mary		5		
Cranshaw	James		6m		
Cattrall	James	F			
Cattrall	Betty	M			
Cattrall	Mary				
Cureden	Henry		42		
Cureden	Betty		33		5
Cureden	Henry		70		
Cureden	Elizabeth		70		
Craven	Nancy		30		
Cureden	James		18		
Callison	Ester	M		Stanley St	
Callison	Sarah		14		
Cliff	William		+		
Cliff	Ann				
Cliff	John		10		
Cliff	Thos		3		
Crumbleholme	Wm				
Councal	Dolley	M			
Counsal	Lawrance		11		
Connal	Willm	F		Bridge St	
Connal	Ann	M			
Connal	Mary		38		
Connal	Elling		30		
Connal	-		10		
Connal	Joseph		5		
Connal	W				
Connal	Miles		13		
Connal	Jane		1		
Calling	John	F			

1810 Census   Catholic Congregation of Preston

Surname	Forename(s)	Rel	Age	Address	Comm
Calling	Alice	M			
Calling	Margret		13		
Calling	Elizth		9		
Calling	Richard		5		
Calling	Christopher		1		
Clifton	Lord				
Clifton	Lady				
Coupe	John	F			
Coupe	Ellen	M			
Coupe	Sare				
Curden	Mathew	F			
Curden	Ester	M			
Curden	Henry		19		
Curden	Mathew		7		
Curden	Richd		5		
Curden	Mary		4		
Curden	Ester		2		
Cooper	Henry			Friergate	
Cooper	Widdow				
Carter	James	F			
Carter	Alice	M			
Carter	Ann		14		
Carter	Mary		12		
Carter	Dorothy		10		
Carter	Robert		8		
Carter	Richd		6		
Carter	Elling		2		
Clayton	Nick	F		Back Lane	
Clayton	Margret	M			
Clayton	Ann		18+		
Clayton	Dolley		16+		
Clayton	Catherine		14+		
Clayton	Margery		12		
Clayton	Henry		9		
Clayton	Richd		7		
Clayton	John		4		
Clayton	Willm		2		
Clayton	James				
Charnley	Miss				
Cureden	Margret			Frirg	
Crumbleholme	Widdow				
Councal	Dolly				
Councal	Lawrance		11		
Cambel	Widdow	M		Sing row	
Cambel	John		11		
Cambel	Margret		6		
Cureden	Elizth		17	Frirg	
Cooper	Elling				
Cooper	Robt				
Carlile	John			Sing	

1810 Census   Catholic Congregation of Preston

Surname	Forename(s)	Rel	Age	Address	Comm
Carlile	Mary				
Coup	Henry	F			
Coup	Matty	M			
Coup	Robt		15		
Coup	Mary		12		
Coil	Susanah		8		
Curden	John	F			
Curden	Jinney	M			
Curden	Betty		4		
Curden	Thos		3m		
Corcorcan	Patrick	F		br St	
Corcorcan	Frances	M			
Corcorcan	Thos		12		
Corcorcan	Nancy		6		
Corcorcan	Nicholas		6		
Corcorcan	Mary		18m		6
Dalton	John Esqr	F		Wnkly Place	
Dalton	Mary	M			
Dalton	Mary		+		
Dalton	Lucy		+		
Dalton	Eliz		+		
Dalton	Bridget		+		
Dunderdale	Robt	F		Spit M	
Dunderdale	Jane	M			
Dunderdale	Richd		+		
Dunderdale	John		+		
Dunderdale	Mary		+		
Dunderdale	Robt		5		
Dunderdale	Jane		2		
Diggles	Wm	F			
Diggles	Betty	M			
Diggles	John		14		
Diggles	Jane		+		
Diggles	Betty		13		
Diggles	Margery		9		
Darlington	Nancy			Vicar St	
Darlington	Agnes		4		
Darlington	Marg		1		
Donelly	Charles				
Donelly	Sar				
Dickenson	John			Feeble St	
Dickenson	Marg		3		
Dickenson	Betty		1		
Davies	Helen	Wd		Syke	
Diggles/Goodear	John O	F			
Diggles	Mary	M			
Davies	James	F		Blue Bell Yd	
Davies	Patience	M			
Davies	Margaret		5		
Davies	Edward			Cch St	

1810 Census   Catholic Congregation of Preston

Surname	Forename(s)	Rel	Age	Address	Comm
Danniel	Joseph				
Duffy	Francis			Ribbleton Lane	
Devehelland	Francis			Ribbleton Lane	
Duckworth	Esther			Cch St	
Dewhirst	Joseph				
	Ann				
Dodds	Joseph	F			
	Elizabeth	M			
	Mary				
	Elizabeth				
Dewhurst	James		36	Walton St	
	Alice		33		
	Richd		10		
	Jemima		6		
	Margaret		5		
	James		3		
Darlington	Nancy	M		Vicar St	
	Agnes		4		
	Margaret		1		
Donelly	Charles		+		
	Sarah				
Dickinson	John	F		Fable St	
	Margaret		3		
	Betty		1		
Dewherst	Hewgh		64	Ld St	
Darren	Edward			Stanley St	
Darren	Alice				
Darren	Ellen		14		
Darren	Ann		8		
Darren	Willm		5		
Darren	James		1		
Dilworth	John		14	Holden Square	
Dilworth	Ann		12		
Dilworth	Thos		9		
Dilworth	Henry		7		
Dilworth	George		5		
Dagon	John		5		
Dewhurst	Peeter	F		Heatley St	
Dewhurst	John		4		
Dewhurst	Richd		2		
Duckworth	John				
Duckworth	Jane				
Dewhurst	Cathrine	M			
Dewhurst	Elizabeth		13x		
Darbishire	Widow				
Dobson	Henry			Heatley St	
Darbishire	Jenney			Sing	
Dunderdil	Alice				
Dunderdil	Mary		29		
Dewhurst	John	F			

1810 Census — Catholic Congregation of Preston

Surname	Forename(s)	Rel	Age	Address	Comm
Dewhurst	Alice	M			
Dewhurst	Richard		4		
Dewhurst	Ann		2		
Dickinson	James	F			
Dickinson	Matty	M			
Dickinson	Betty		19		
Dickinson	Ann		18		
Dickinson	James		11		
Dickinson	Peeter		7		
Dickinson	Willm		5		
Dickinson	Thos		2		
Dickinson	John	F			
Dickinson	Ellen	M			
Dickinson	Nancy		18		
Dickinson	Mary		17		
Dickinson	John		15		
Dickinson	Margt		13		
Dickinson	Ellen		10		
Dickinson	Betty		7		
Dickinson	Willm		4		
Dickinson	Alice		6m		
Dilworth	Willm		6		
Dilworth	Margery		3		
Dunderdil	Ann	M			
Dunderdil	Bellow				
Dunderdil	Sarah		16x		
Dunderdil	Richd		14		
Dunderdil	Mary		11		
Dagger	Ann	M			
Dagger	Ellen		10		
Dagger	Jady		3		
Dagger	John		1		
Dobson	Lawrance	F		High St	
Dobson	Margret	M			
Dobson	Ellen		18		
Dobson	Ann		11		
Dobson	John		7		
Dobson	Mary		1		
Dawson	James	F			
Dawson	Betty	M			
Dawson	Joseph		6		
Dawson	Margret		3		
Dawson	Richd		1		
Duckit	Richd	F			
Ducket	Mary	M			
Ducket	Thos		6		
Ducket	James		1		
Dobson	Mary	M			
Dobson	Mary		x		
Dilworth	Joseph	F			

1810 Census   Catholic Congregation of Preston

Surname	Forename(s)	Rel	Age	Address	Comm
Dilworth	Alice	M			
Dilworth	Thos		14		
Dilworth	Mary		11		
Dilworth	John		10		
Dilworth	Henry		8		
Elinthorp	John	F		Hgh St	
Elinthorp	Margt				
Elinthorp	Wm		2		
Elinthorp	Tho		1		
Eastham	Edmund		78		
Easterby	Isabella	M		Mount St	
Easterby	Richard		6		
Easterby	Mary		4		
Eastwood	Frances Mary				
Eccles	Margaret			Cch St	
English	Edward			Ribbleton Lane	
Eastham	Mrs			Park C	
Eastwood	John	F			
	Elling	M			
	Ann				
	Mary				
	William		12		
	George		10		
	Ralph		1		
Eccleston	Edmund				
Edmundson	Ellen			Whittaker Row	
Eccles	Mathew	F			
Eccles	Nancy	M			
Eccles	John		17x		
Eccles	James		15x		
Eccles	Lawrance		8		
Eccles	Ann		4		
Eastam	Richard	F		Hutton	
Eastam	Agness	M			
Eastam	Thomas		8		
Eastam	Betty		6	and	
Eastam	Elling		4		
Eastam	Lawrance		1	Longton	
Eastam	Thomas	F	32	Ld St	
Eastam	Mary	M	36		
Eastam	John		14		
Eastam	Thos		7		
Eastam	George		5		
Eccleston	Mrs			Leeming St	
Eccleston	Ann				
Eaves	Mary	M			
Eaves	Oswl		8		
Eaves	Ann		5		
Eaves	Agness		2		

24

1810 Census   Catholic Congregation of Preston

Surname	Forename(s)	Rel	Age	Address	Comm
Edminson	Mary				7
Fletcher	Mary			Hg St	
Flint	Crist				
Flint	Betty				
Flint	James				
Fishwick	Rob	F			
	Ann		19		
	John		14		
	Rob		11		
	Marg		9		
Fazekerly	Jas	F		Wlker St	
	Ann	M			
	Alice		x		
	Jane				
	Marg		+		
	Mary		12		
	Jas		9		
	Ann		2		
Faith	Bella				
Fisher	Alice			Moor l	
Fellows	Cicily	Sv		Fishg	
Fowler	Jane L			Rose St	
Freed	Henry			Cch St	
Fawcet	Joseph	F		Stanley St	
"	Sarah				
Fryer	Felix	F		Mt St	
Fryer	Frances	M			
	Betty				
	Margaret				
Fox	Betty				
Frost	George				
Flannagan	Edward				
Forniford	William	F		near Vicar St	
	Ellin	M			
	Mary		10		
	Elizabeth		8		
	Margaret		6		
	Ellin		1		
Flitcroft	Ann	M			
	Mary		9		
	Nancy		7		
Fazisackly	Ellen	M			
Fazisackly	John		8		
Foss	Walter	F	32	Ld St	
Foss	Mary	M	33		
Foss	Joseph		4		
Foss	Betty		1		
Fayle	Ruth	M	47		
Fayle	Charity		19		
Fayle	Henry		17		

25

1810 Census   Catholic Congregation of Preston

Surname	Forename(s)	Rel	Age	Address	Comm
Fayle	Willm		14		
Fayle	Eliz		6		
Fisher	Ann		55		
Finch	Betty	M		Queen St	
Finch	Sally				
Foard	Ann	M			
Foard	Betty		15		
Foard	Mary		14		
Foard	Joseph		12		
Foard	-		10		
Fellows	James			Bridge St	
Fellows	Margret	M			
Fellows	Henry	F			
Fellows	Mary	M			
Fellows	John		10		
Fellows	Ann		6		
Fellows	Mary		3		
Fellows	Henry				
Foster	Jane	M		Lills Yard	
Foster	Elling		9		
Foster	Elizabeth		5		
Gillibrand	Mrs			Fsh	
Grundy	Ann	Sv			
Gerard	Mrs				
Glover	Mrs				
Gillow	Rob	F			
Gillow	Mary	M			
Gillow	Rob		2		
Gillow	Eliz		1		
Gibson	Mary	Sv			
Greaves	Thos			Ever G	
Gaving	John			Hgh S	
Gaving	Cath				
	Bryan				
	Winif				
Greenhalgh	Ann				
Grundy	Robt	F		Cnl St	
	Mary	M			
	Wm	S	1		
Goodear	John	F			
	Betty	M			
Grayston	Wm	F			
	Ann	M			
	John		13+		
	Margt		10		
	Wm		7		
	Jos		2		
Gregson	Tho	F			
	Mary	M			
	John		14		

1810 Census　　　　Catholic Congregation of Preston

Surname	Forename(s)	Rel	Age	Address	Comm
[Gregson]	Wm		12		
	Peter		10		
	Thos		6		
	Jas		4		
	Ann		2		
Gradwell	Mr			Ld St	
	Mrs				
	John Jnr				
	George				
	Ann		14		
Gillow	James	F		Cch St	
	Mary	M			
	Thomas		7		
	Mary		2		
Groce	Thomas	F		Lds Factory	
	Mary				
Gregson	William		21	Cch St	
Gillatt	Jane			Mt St	
Gillatt	Richd				
Graveling	Mary				
Guest	Mary				
Gregson	Thos				
Garrade	Lady				
Gornal	Agnes			Cch St	
Gillow	James	F		Cch St	
	Mary	M			
	Thomas		7		
	Mary		2		
Gornall	Peter			Ribbleton Lane	
Gartley	Michael			Ribbleton Lane	8
Gardner	Henry		27	Park l	
Gardner	Jane		25		
Gardner	Mary		40		
Glover	Joseph		45	Ch St	
Glover	Ellen		40		
Grundy	William O		35		
Gardner	Mary	M	40	Dale	
Gardner	Nicholas		10		
Grimbaldeston	Mrs		50		
Gradwell	Alice				
Gregson	Thos	F		Starch house	
	Alice	M			
	William		+		
	John		+		
	Mary		12		
	George		8		
	James		5		
Gregson	George	F	+		
	Alice	M	+		
	Ellin		11		

1810 Census   Catholic Congregation of Preston

Surname	Forename(s)	Rel	Age	Address	Comm
[Gregson]	William		7		
	George		5		
	John		3		
	Betty		1		
Goodier	Ellin			Snow Hill	
Goss	Catherine			Fable St	
Grayston	John	Hu			
Grayston	Jane	Wf			
Grimston	Robt		18	Ld St	
Gregson	Mrs			Leeming St	
Green	Betty				
Goodear	Betty	M		Queen St	
Goodear	Ellen		14		
Goodear	Willm		12		
Gregson	Robert		60		
Gregson	Betty		60		
Gregson	Mary		28		
Gregson	John		25		
Gardener	Mary	M		Houlding Sqe	
Gardner	James		18		
Gardner	Willm		16		
Gardner	Thos		14		
Gardner	Edward		12		
Gardner	Richard		10		
Gardner	Joseph		7		
Grime	Catherine				
Gredgson	Henry	F		Bridget St	
Gredgson	Mary	M			
Gredgson	Jane		14x		
Gredgson	Richd		9		
Gredgson	Thos		5		
Gredson	John		3		
Grunday	James			Friergate	
Grunday	Margret				
Gradwell	John				
Gradwell	Mary	Wf			
Gradwell	John	F		Friergate	
Gradwell	Jane	M			
Gradwell	Willm		20		
Gradwell	James		29		
Gradwell	Catherine		16		
Gould	James	F		Back Lane	
Gould	Mary	M			
Gould	Mary		23x		
Gould	Elizth		22x		
Gould	Ann		21x		
Gould	John		16x		
Gould	Margret		14x		
Gould	Jane		12		
Goodear	Joseph			Sing	

1810 Census   Catholic Congregation of Preston

Surname	Forename(s)	Rel	Age	Address	Comm
Goodear	Margt				
Gregson	Edward	F			
Gregson	Ann		18		
Gregson	John		11		
Gregson	Geo				
Gooder	Willm	F			
Gooder	Betty	M			
Gooder	John		15		
Goodear	Betty		13		
Gooder	Margery		6		
Gooder	Joseph	F			
Gooder	Ester	M			
Gooder	John		14		
Gooder	Betty		12		
Gooder	Betty		7		
Grundy	Alice	M			
Grundy	Bellow		23		
Grundy	Alice		12		
Grundy	Charles		9		
Grundy	Edward		7		
Grundy	Richd		4		
Gillet	Nicholas				
Hardman	Ric		7 ?	Dale St	
	Jane		15		
	Rob		14		
	John		12		
	Margaret		9		
	James		4		
	Wm		3		
Hornby	Helen		+2		
	Jas		15		
	Wm		6		
Holiday	Joshua O		19		
Helm	John		+3		
	Anne		+		
	Jas		14		
	Wm		12		
	Elizab		5		
Hardman	Peter				
	Elizab		+8		
	Mary		18		
	Margaret		14		
	Joan		12		
	John		10		
	Anne		8		
	Hannah		7		
	Elizab				
	Alice				
	Isabella				
Hawker	Elizab			Holden Square	

1810 Census   Catholic Congregation of Preston

Surname	Forename(s)	Rel	Age	Address	Comm
Helm	Thos		+6	Stanley St	
	Anne		+		
	Jas		15		
	John		12		
	Geo		10		
	Jane		9		
	Margaret		7		
	Joseph		1		
Haggers	Thos		+		
	Margaret		+		
Hothersall	Betty	M		Queen Str	
	John	S			
Holmes	Matthew	F			
	Grace	M			
	Thos		9		
Holmes	Dorothy		7		
Holmes	Robt		4m		
Higginson	Ann	Sv		Ch St	9
Heywood	William			Rose St	
	Hellen	M			
	Hellen		4		
	Dorothy		1		
Harris	Mary			Chh St	
Heatley	John			Chh St	
Heatley	Mrs				
Heatley	Peter		Inf		
Horrocks	Ann	Sv	18		
Hibbert	Nathan	F			
	Anne	M			
	Anne		11		
	James		5		
Hubberstey	Joseph		28	Chh St	
Hubberstey	Thomas		24		
Harrison	Betty		20	Grimshaw St	
Hall	Mary	M			
	Ann		12		
	Ellen		7		
	Betty		6		
Harrison	Mary	M		Cch St	
	Jane				
	Margaret				
	Nancy		11		
Heatley	John	F		Cch St	
	Mary	M			
	Peter		1		
Howarth	John (Asst)				
Hull	George			Ribbleton Lane	
	Margaret				
Holding	George	F		Ribbleton Lane	8
	Jane	M			

1810 Census   Catholic Congregation of Preston

Surname	Forename(s)	Rel	Age	Address	Comm
[Holding]	Richd		8		
	William		4		
	Grace		1		
Hartley	James		23	Chh	
Hartley	Ellen		25		
Hartley	Nanny		7		
Harrison	Abraham		50		
Harrison	Grace		40		
Harrison	Dolly		14		
Harrison	Betty		30		
Harrison	Betty		6		
Harrison	Jane		2		
Hunt	Richd		40		
Hunt	Nancy		35		
Hunt	William		10		
Holland	John		13?	Park C	
Holland	James		11		
Holland	James		6		
Harrison	James	F	38	Chtte	
Harrison	Nancy	M	30		
Harrison	Thos		11		
Harrison	John		9		
Harrison	Mary		5		
Harrison	Edward		1		
Holderness	William	F	60		
Holderness	Alice	M	60		
Holderness	George		25		
Holderness	Jane		25		
Harrison	John	F	25		
Harrison	Peggy	M	29		
Harrison	Thos		7		
Harrison	Dolly		5		
Helme	Nanny		22	(Cottam)	
Helme	Jane		13		
Helme	Betty		11		
Helme	Robert		8		
Hall	William	F			
	Elling	M			
	James		10		
Hornby	William				
Hall	Betty				
	Ann				
Hodgon	Isabella				
	Thomas				
Hall	Dorothy		47	Vauxhall Road	
	Margaret		8		
Hatch	Thomas	F	+	Vicar St	
	William		+		
	Margaret		+		
	Thomas		14		

1810 Census   Catholic Congregation of Preston

Surname	Forename(s)	Rel	Age	Address	Comm
Hatch	William		+	Starch h	
Houghton	Evan	F	+	near Vicar St	
	Margaret	M	+		
	Lettice		19		
	William		17		
	Ellin		9		
	Mary		4		
Holmes	Richard	F	+		
	Ann	M	+		
	Betty		5		
	James		3		
Hays	Christopher	F	+		
	Betty	M	+		
	Betty		+		
	Jane		+		
	Thos		13		
	Mary		7		
Higginson	William	F	+		
	Ellin	M	+		
	Betty		8		
	William		5		
	Sarah		1		
Hart	Michael	F	+		
	Jane	M	+		
	Jane		2		
Holliday	Peter		+	Snow Hill	
	Ann		+		
Heys	Ellin	M	+		
	Jane		6		
	John		2		
Helme	Thomasing	M		Qn St	
	Ann		0		
	John				
	Margt				
	William		10		
	James		7		
Holliday	John	F		Qn St	
	William		8		
	Betty		6		
	George		2		
Harrison	Richard	F			
	Alice	M			
	Abraham		3		
Higgins	Patrick	F		Leeming St	
	Ann	M			
	Margt				
	Agnes				
	John				
Hall	Esther				
Holderness	Alice	M			

1810 Census — Catholic Congregation of Preston

Surname	Forename(s)	Rel	Age	Address	Comm
[Holderness]	William				
	Margt				
	Joseph				
	Ann				
	Peter				
Helme	Richard				
Haydock	Christopher				
Holderness	Betty	M			
	Mary		7		
	Margt		5		
	John		3		
Hindle	Mary	M			
	William				
	John				
Hile	Richard	F			
	Betty	M			
	Sally				
	Jane				
	Betty				
	Dorothy				
	Hannah				
	Thomas				
Hall	Widow	M		Heatley St	
	Edwd		12		
	William		10		
	Margt		6		
	Elizth		4		
	Patience				
Hogson	James	F		Trc G	
	Jane	M			
	Thomas		14		
	John		10		
Hubberstey	Henry				
	Jane				
Howarth	Mary	M			
	Margt		5		
	Robert		3		
	John		1		
Hardman	James	F			
	Ann	M			
	Ann		12		
	James		1		
Hoole	Widow				
Hacking	John	F			
	Elizth	M			
	Catherine		10		
	Cicely		9		
	James		7		
	William		1		
Hurst	Christopher	F			

1810 Census　　　　　　　　Catholic Congregation of Preston

Surname	Forename(s)	Rel	Age	Address	Comm
[Hurst]	Ruth	M			
	Mary		21		
	Christopher		15		
	Thos		8		
	Ellin		6		
	Ann		4		
Hargreaves	Widow	M			
	Ann				
Higginson	John	F			
	Mary	M			
	Ann		5		
Hilton	Widow			Brg St	
Hudson	Ann				
Hardman	Willm	F			
Hardman	Mary	M			
Hardman	Bridget		10		
Hardman	Robt		7		
Hardman	Mary				
Hool	Mathew	F			
Hool	Betty	M			
Hool	George		19		
Hool	Peggy		17		
Hool	William		12		
Hool	Robert		8		
Hool	Betty		3		
Hargreaves	Catherine			Tythe Barn St	
Holmes	Betty	M		Whittaker Row	
Holmes	Ellen		14		
Holmes	Betty		x		
Holmes	Alice		12		
Holmes	Mary		8		
Holliday	George	Hu	55	Back Lane	
Holliday	Betty	Wf	50		
Holmes	Robert	Hu	65		
Holmes	Betty	Wf	68		
Hall	John	Sv	15	Ld St	
Henry	Hugh	F	35	Shambles	
Henry	Mary	M	38		
Henry	Elling		14		
Henry	Mary		7		
Henry	Hugh		5		
Henry	Joseph		3		
Henry	Elizabeth		1		
Hubersty	Thos	F	50		
Hubersty	Ellen	M	47		
Hubersty	James		19		
Hubersty	Thomas		10		
Hubersty	William		8		
Higgison	James		25		
Higginson	Matty		22		5

1810 Census   Catholic Congregation of Preston

Surname	Forename(s)	Rel	Age	Address	Comm
Hornby	Richard		40		
Hatch	John		44		
Hatch	Grace		38		
Hatch	Catherine		20		
Hatch	Mary		18		
Hatch	Elling		16		
Hatch	Sarrah		14		
Hatch	Ann		12		
Hatch	Alice		8		
Hatch	Elizth		5		
Hatch	James		2		
Harrison	Betty		60		
Hurst	Nancy		50		
Hornby	John		50		
Hudson	Ann				
Highton	Alice	M			
Houlding	Edward	F			
Houlden	Ann	M			
Harrison	Betty	M			
Harrison	Ann		12		
Hornby	Thos				
Hornby	Betty				
Hall	Mary				
Houlins	Willm				
Houlins	Elling				
Houghton	Edwd	F			
Houghton	Elling	M			
Houghton	William		8		
Houghton	Betty		6		
Houghton	John		4		
Houghton	Thos		2		
Holton	Willm	F			
Holton	Sarah	M			
Holton	Geo		1		
Houghton	Sarah	M			
Houghton	Mary				
Houlden	Edward				
Houlden	Mary				
Houlden	Willm				
Houlden	Eling				
Harrison	John	F			
Harrison	Catherine	M			
Harrison	Ann		18x		
Harrison	Jane		17x		
Harrison	Mary		12x		
Harrison	Betty		11		
Harrison	Agness		9		
Harrison	Elling		6		
Holden	James				
Harrison	Betty	M			

1810 Census   Catholic Congregation of Preston

Surname	Forename(s)	Rel	Age	Address	Comm
Harrison	Mary		6		
Horrobin	Geo	F			
Horrobin	Mary	M			
Horrobin	Geo		7		
Horrobin	Richd		5		
Horrobin	Ann		5		
Horrobin	Mary		1		
Horrobin	Betty		1		
Hardicer	Lucke	F			
Hardicar	Sissaly	M			
Hardicar	Deberah		14		
Hardicar	Willm		1		
Holland	Margery	M			
Holland	Margret		x		
Holland	"		13		
Holland	Richard		10		
Hadock	Geo	F			
Hadock	Thos		6		
Hadock	Willm		4		
Hadock	Mary		1		
Higginson	Willm				
Heays	Ann	M			
Heays	Margret		8		
Heays	Mary		1		
Higginson	Mary	M		More Lane	
Higganson	Willm		11		
Higginson	Betty		9		
Higginson	Mary		7		
Harrison	John	F			
Harrison	Margt	M			
Harrison	Ann		x		
Harrison	Thos		19x		
Harrison	Alice		17x		
Harrison	John		15		
Harrison	Margt		13		
Harrison	James		10		
Harrison	David		9		
Harrison	Mary		7		
Harrison	Ellen		.6		
Harrison	Ewd		3		
Harrison	Joseph		1		
Houlden	Richd	F			
Houlden	Jane	M			
Houlden	Jane		20		
Houlden	James		10		
Houlden	Richd		6		
Houlden	Henry		4		
Houghton	Alice	M			
Houghton	Elling		16x		
Houghton	Ann		12		

1810 Census   Catholic Congregation of Preston

Surname	Forename(s)	Rel	Age	Address	Comm
Houghton	Betty		11		
Houghton	Willm		5		
Houghton	Ann		3		
Helmn	John	F			
Helmn	Ann	M			
Helmn	Mary		3		
Helmn	Willm		1		
Hall	Lawrance	F			
Hall	Elling	M			
Hall	Robt		12		
Hall	Elling		10		
Hall	Ann		6		
Hall	Margret		1		
Ibison	Cath	Sv		Fishg	
Jackson	William	F		John St	
	Elizabeth	M			
	Anne		3		
	John		1		
Jackson	George				
Johnson	Betty	Sv	23		
Johnson	Betty			Cch St	
Johnson	John		22	Vauxhall Road	
	Mary		20		
Irving	Hannah	M			
	John		16		
	Betty		6		
Jackson	William	F		St John St	
Jackson	Betty	M			
Jackson	Nancy		3		
Jackson	John		1		
Johnson	Margret	Sv	13	Ld St	
Jamison	John		30		
Jamison	Elling		27		
Jackson	Widdow			friergate	
Jackson	George		24		
Jackson	Jane		22		
Jones	Jane		14		
Justy	John		3		
Juste	Vincent				
Justi	Ann		3		10
Jackson	Willm				
Jackson	Kitty				
Johnson	James	F		Everton Gardens	
Johnson	Alice	M			
Johnson	Margt		13		
Johnson	Jane		11		
Johnson	James Alxd		7		
Johnson	Robt		3		
Johnson	Mary		1		
Kenyon	Betty	M		Moor l	

1810 Census   Catholic Congregation of Preston

Surname	Forename(s)	Rel	Age	Address	Comm
Kenyon	Ann		11		
Kenyon	Wm		5		
Kenyon	Heny		3		
Knight	Alice		74	Ch St	
Kitchen	John	F		Sch St	
	Anne	M			
	Mary		2		
	William		Inf		
Knowle	John		12	Ch St	
Kellie	William	F			11
	Sarah	M			
	Susan		2		
Kilshaw	Alice				
Kay	Wm	F			
Kay	Betty	M			
Kay	John		2		
Keary	Georgina				
Kay	Robt	F			
Kay	Margaret	M			
Kay	James		7		
Kay	Richard		6		
Kay	Mary		2		
Kay	Robt		1		
Kay	George		x		
Kellet	Robt	F			
Kellet	Betty	M			
Kellet	Ann		x		
Kitchen	Henry	F			
Kitchen	Betty	M			
Kitchen	Mary		1		
Kay	Susannah	M			
Kay	Nancy	D			
Kay	Susannah		5		
Kay	William		27	Longton	
Kitchen	Robt		x	Stanley St	
Kitchen	Thos		15		
Kitchen	Ester		10		
Kitchen	John		7		
Kitchen	Mary		4		
Kenyon	James				
Kenyon	Ellen				
Kenyon	Jane		15		
Kenyon	Mary		11		
Kilshaw	Joseph	F		Heatley St	
Kilshaw	Elizth	M			
Kilshaw	Jane		13		
Kilshaw	Henry		7		
Kitchin	Hennry	F		friergate	
Kitchin	Jane	M			
Kitchin	Richd		23		

1810 Census   Catholic Congregation of Preston

Surname	Forename(s)	Rel	Age	Address	Comm
Kitchin	Joseph		18		
Kitchin	Margret		9		
Kurden	Mary				
Kurden	Elizth		13		
Kurden	Sarah		4		
Koil	Susanah				
Koil	Mathew	F			
Koil	Martha	M			
Koil	Margt		8		
Kooper	Betty				
Kay	William				
Kay	Alice				
Kay	John				
Kay	Ester				
Kay	Peeter		29		
Kay	Alice		19		
Kay	Nancy		15		
Kay	Willm		12		
Kay	Andrew		9		
Kay	John		1		
Kay	Sarah				
Lancl	Rev Monsr			Fishg	
Lonsdale	Helen	Sv			
Lawson	Robt	F			
	Bella	M			
	Wm	S	5		
	John	S	2		
Lever	John	F		Rose St	
	Betty	M			
	Robert		7		
	Jane		13		
	Alice		2		
Leyfield	Edward	F		Lib St	
	Anne	M			
	Margt		16		
	Anne		6		
Lea	Porter			Ch St	12
Lund	Mrs			Ch St	13
Livesey	George	F		near Blue Bell	
	Helen	M			
	Catherine		16		
	Helen		12		
	Thomas		9		
	Roger		7		
	Mary		5		
	George		3		
	Margaret		1		
Lea	Alice				
Lancaster	Elizabeth			Cch St	
Loftus	Ellen		29	Ch Ln	

1810 Census　　　　　Catholic Congregation of Preston

Surname	Forename(s)	Rel	Age	Address	Comm
Livesey	John	F	50		
Livesey	Betty	M	40		
Livesey	Richd		16		
Livesey	Margt		8		
Livesey	Betty		7		
Livesey	William		5		
Lofthouse	James				
Latham	Randle				
Latus	Joseph	F			
Latus	Mary	M			
Latus	Mary		8		
Latus	James		6		
Latus	Ellen		4		
Latus	Ann		2		
Leach	Richd	F			
Leach	Betty	M			
Leach	Margaret		11		
Leach	Nancy		8		
Leach	Betty		6		
Leach	Lucy		3		
Lucas	Thos	F		Qun St	
	Martha	M			
	Thos		21		
	Jane		16		
	Lawe		14		
	Bello		9		
	Elling		6		
	John		4		
	Hannah		1		
Leigh	William				
	Margt				
Leigh	Thos	F			
	Mary	M			
	Peter				
	David				
	James				
	Michael				
Layland	Alice	M			
Layland	John		3		
Livsey	John	F		Back Lane	
Livsey	Hannah	M			
Livsey	Catherine		3		
Livsey	Mary		1		
Lee	Richard		x	Vicar St	
Livsey	Jane		60	Hutton	
Luckes	William	F			
Luckes	Ann		23		
Luckes	William		19	and	
Luckes	Robert		14		
Luckes	John		11	Longton	

1810 Census   Catholic Congregation of Preston

Surname	Forename(s)	Rel	Age	Address	Comm
Leeming	Mrs	M	30	Ld St	
Leeming	Mary		11		
Leeming	Bridget		9		
Leeming	Margret		7		
Leeming	James		5		
Livsey	Ann			qu lane?	14
Lofthouse	Elizth	M	55	Areton wiend	
Lofthouse	John		20		
Lambert	Michal			Dale St	
Lambert	Rosenna				
Lambert	James		14		
Lambert	Richard		11		
Lambert	William		8		
Lambert	Rosenna				
Livesey	Willm	F		Dale St	
Livesey	Ellen	M			
Livesey	Mary		27		
Livesey	Betty		24		
Livesey	Ann		21		
Livesey	Thos		17		
Livesey	Joseph		10		
Livesey	John		7		
Livesey	Peeter		2		
Lester	Patrick			Stanley St	
Lester	Ann				
Lester	John		6		
Lester	Ann		8		
Lester	Dan?		4		
Lester	Alice		2		
Latus	Willm	F		Briget St	
Latus	Mary	M			
Latus	Mary		17x		
Latus	John		15x		
Leach	James	F		frierg	
Leach	Sarah	M			
Leach	Richd		16x		
Leach	Willm		15x		
Leach	Thomasin		9		
Leach	John		6		
Leach	Mary		3		
Longtry	John		2		
Longtry	Peeter		10		
Lancaster	Alce				
Leeming	Jane				
Leeming	Sarah				
Layfield	Thos				
Layfield	Betty				
Leech	Ann	M			
Leech	Margt		3		
Leech	Mary		x		

1810 Census   Catholic Congregation of Preston

Surname	Forename(s)	Rel	Age	Address	Comm
Leech	Ellin		x		
Leech	Joseph				
Longtree	John				
Lontree	Mary				
Latus	Betty				
Livsey	Willm	F		Walker St	
Livsey	Betty	M			
Livsey	Robt		14		
Livsey	Willm		11		
Livsey	Elling		8		
Livsey	Nicholas		6		
Livsey	James		1		
Layfield	John	F			
Layfield	Alice		16		
Layfield	Alice	M			
Lund	Robt	F			
Lund	Margret	M			
Lund	John				
Lund	Betty				
Lund	James		12		
Lund	Thos		17x		
Leeming	John				
Lancaster	Geo	F			
Lancaster	Margt	M			
Lancaster	Mary		14		
Lancaster	Margt		13		
Lancaster	Richd		9		
Lancaster	Betty		7		
Lancaster	Lucy		5		
Lancaster	Agness		3		
Laytham	Nancy	M			
Laytham	Mary		21		
Laytham	Margt		11		
Laytham	Juliana		10		
Layfield	Mary				
Layfield	Alice		6		
Layfield	Ann		3		
Luvett	Joseph				
Luvett	Mary				
Lund	Antony	F			
Lund	Margt	M			
Lund	John		2		
Leech	Willm	F			
Leech	Ann	M			
Leech	James		12		
Leech	Margt		10		
Leech	John		9		
Leech	Ellen		8		
Leech	Charles		6		
Leech	Richd		2		

1810 Census — Catholic Congregation of Preston

Surname	Forename(s)	Rel	Age	Address	Comm
Monkhouse	Ann	Sv			
Mayor	Peggy	M			
	Mary	D	9		
	Cath	D	7		
Mather	Elizth	Sv	16	Lib St	
May	John		64	Chh St	
	Mrs				
Marsh	Elizabeth				
Macneal	James	F			
	Bello	St			
	William		16		
	Mary		14		
	Thomas		12		
	Paul		9		
Mason	Ann				
Mason	Mary				
Marlow	Mary				
Mayor	Betty	M			
Melling	Thomasing				
McCan	Francis	F		Ribbleton Lane	
	Rosy	M			
	John		13		
	Barnaby		11		
	Patrick		7		
	Mary		4		
	Elling		2		
Meccune	Hugh			Ribbleton Lane	
	Dorothy				
Moore	Francis			Cch St	
Marsh	James		38	Kg	
Marsh	Betty		30		
Moss	John		12	Chltte S	
Margerison	Richd		60		
Margerison	Alice		60		
Mackerall	Richd	F	37	Kg	
Mackerall	Ellin	M	37		
Mackerall	James		13		
Mackerall	Mary		6		
Mackerall	Betty		2		
Moreley	Robt	F	29	Dk St	
Moreley	Alice		29		
Moreley	Mary		5		
Moreley	Betty		3		
Mason	Elizabeth				
Myers	Nancy				
Melling	Joseph				
Melling	Alice				
Mountsey	Mary	M			
Mountsey	Bello		+		
Mountsey	George		12		

1810 Census   Catholic Congregation of Preston

Surname	Forename(s)	Rel	Age	Address	Comm
Mountsey	Nancy		9		
Mountsey	Joseph		5		
Moor	Thomas				
Moor	Alice				
Miller	Ellen	M			
	Alice	D	24		
	James		14		
Midghall	Richd	F			
	Mary	M			
	Jas		23		
	Ann		20		
	Mary		18		
	Jane		16		
	Cathe		14		
	Hannah		10		
	Henry		12		
	Betty		7		
	Richd		6m		
Morley	James	F			
Morley	Mary	M			
Morley	Jane		20x		
Morley	James		18		
Morley	Betty		14		
Morley	Peggy		12		
Morley	William		10		
Morley	Nancy		10		
Marsden	John	F			
Marsden	Betty	M			
Marsden	Betty		17		
Marsden	Ellen		16		
Marsden	Robert		4		
Marsden	Ann		2		
Margeson	Thomas	F			
Margeson	Betty	M			
Margeson	John		13		
Margeson	Richard		7		
Margeson	Mary		6		
Margeson	Alice		5		
Margeson	Bellow		5		
Margeson	Betty		2		
Margeson	Thomas		1		
Moon	John	F			
Moon	Mary	M			
Moon	Nancy		6		
Moon	Betty		4		
Moon	Mathew		2		
Miller	Rodger	F		Vicar St	
Miller	Elling	M			
Miller	Alice		4		
Miller	Elling		2		

1810 Census — Catholic Congregation of Preston

Surname	Forename(s)	Rel	Age	Address	Comm
Moss	Elling			Feble St	
Moss	Thomas	F		Hutton	
Moss	Alice	M			
Moss	James		17		
Moss	Richard		11		
Moss	Thomas		8		
Moss	Joseph		6		
Moss	John	F		and	
Moss	Ann	M		[Longton]	
Moss	Betty		35	Hutton	
Moss	Margret		27		
Moss	Mary		13		
Moss	Janes		2		
Moss	Ralph	F			
Moss	Betty	M			
Moss	Jane		25		
Moss	William		23		
Moss	Elling		17		
Moss	Mary		11	and	
Moss	Thomas	F			
Moss	Ann	M			
Moss	Thomas		17		
Moss	William		16		
Moss	Henry		13		
Moss	John		6		
Moss	James	F			
Moss	Jane	M			
Moss	Betty		11		
Moss	Ann		7		
Moss	Thomas		3		
Moss	Ralph		1	Longton	
Miller	Chrisr			Leeming St	
Miller	Alice				
Miller	Thos				
Miller	Ann				
Miller	Mary				
Moss	Betty	M		Parradice St	
Moss	Jane		7		
Moss	Margret		6m		
Moss	Ann				
Moss	Dory				
Moan	Ann		40		
Moan	James		12		
Morehead	Phillip		22		
Melling	Thos	F		Stanley St	
Melling	Ellen	M			
Melling	Richard		21		
Melling	Thos		19		
Melling	John		17		
Melling	Elling		15		

1810 Census   Catholic Congregation of Preston

Surname	Forename(s)	Rel	Age	Address	Comm
Melling	Joseph	F			
Melling	Ellen	M			
Melling	William				
Melling	James	F			
Melling	Betty	M			
Melling	William		3		
Melling	Joseph		2		
Melling	William				
Melling	Mary				
Magran	Widdow				
Molone	John				
Marsden	Mary			Stanley St	
Morley	W			Heatley St	
Morley	Geo		10		
Melling	James				
Melling	Mary	Wf			
Mascough	John	F		Back Lane	
Mascough	Mary	M			
Mascough	Ann		5		
Mascough	Mary		3		
Mascough	Elling		1		
Micon	Tully				
Mascough	John	F			
Mascough	Richd		27		
Mascough	Rowland		16		
Maden	James	F		Back Lane	
Maden	Dorothy	M			
Maden	Juley		12		
Mercer	James	F			
Mercer	Margret	M			
Mercer	Dorothy		9		
Mercer	Silvester		7		
Mercer	James		5		
Mercer	John		3		
Mercer	Elling		1		
Makings	Hugh				
Marsh	Jhn				
Melling	William		11	Frerg	
Mackenis	Edward	F			
Mackenis	Mary	M			
Mackenis	Margt		8		
Mason	Ann	M			
Mason	Mary		13		
Mason	Ellen		22		
Mason	Nancy		11		
Mason	John		8		
Mason	William		4		
Mackenly	Willm	F			
Mackenaly	Rosy	M			
Mackenaly	Edd		1		

1810 Census — Catholic Congregation of Preston

Surname	Forename(s)	Rel	Age	Address	Comm
Mackenaly	Edd				
Martlon	Geo				
Mutch	Timothy	F			
Mutch	Ellen	M			
Mutch	Christopher		5		
Mutch	Betty		3		
Moss	Peggy	M			
Moss	Thos		8		
Moss	Stephen		7		
Moss	William		5		
Moss	Alice		6m		15
Mackonal	Nancy			Sing	
Macan	John				
Moon	Jane				
Moon	Alice				
Mackneill	Willm		x		
Mighley	Hannah				
Malig	Jane				
Miller	John	F			
Miller	Margret	M			
Miller	Mary		7		
Miller	Thos		5		
Miller	Elling		3		
Miller	Willm		1		
Mcgenley	Michall	F			
Mcgenley	Alice	M			
Mcgenley	John		1		
Morgan	John	F			
Morgan	Ann	M			
Morgan	Ann		4		
Morgan	Rosella		1		
Makning	Daniel	F			
Mackning	Jane	M			
Mackning	Mary		13x		
Mackning	Ann		9		
Mackning	Alexander		3		
Mackning	Daniel		1		
Myerscough	Mary			More Lane	
Morley	Ann				
Naylor	Lewis			Sch St	
	Mary				
Newsham	Thomas			Ch St	
	Agness				
Nangle	Betty	Sv			16
Newsam	James			Mt St	
Newsam	Betty				
Naylor	Mr				
Newsham	John	Sv			1
Nicholson	Thomas	F		Vicar St	
Nicholson	Agness	M			

1810 Census Catholic Congregation of Preston

Surname	Forename(s)	Rel	Age	Address	Comm
Nicholson	Betty		3		
Newsham	Henry			Tythe Barn St	
Noblet	John	F		York St	
Noblet	Sally	M			
Noblet	Thos		18		
Noblet	James		16		
Noblet	Rob		11		
Noblet	Sally		6		
Noblet	Edwd				
Noblet	Joseph		4		
Newbay	Peeter			Stanley St	
Newby	Ellen				
Noblet	Thos				
Noblet	Grace				
Nixson	Robt	F		frierg	
Nixon	Sarah	M			
	Elling	Sv			
Nangles	Ewd	F			
Nangles	Jane	M			
Nangles	Ann		17		
Nangles	Mary		16		
Nangles	James		16		
Nangles	Winifred		9		
Nixon	Christopher	F			
	Elling	M			
	Mary		2		
	Alice		1		
Nixson	William	F			
	Jane	M			
	Agness		7		
	Ann		6		
	Thos		4		
Nobell	Edd	F			
Nobell	John		7		
	George		6		
	Bellow		3		
	Daniall		1		
Noble	Martin				
	Mary				
	Hannah				
Nickson	Joseph	F			
	Mary	M			
	James		x		
	John		x		
	Joseph		x		
	Rebeckah		x		
	Ann		x		
	Mary		x		
Oldham	Betty		Old	Rose St	
Orrell	John				

48

1810 Census — Catholic Congregation of Preston

Surname	Forename(s)	Rel	Age	Address	Comm
Ormond	Dorothy	M			
Ormond	Cuthbert		9		
Owens	Michael	F			
Owens	Nancy	M			
Owens	Michael		10		
Owens	William		7		
Owens	Kitty		4		
Owens	James		2		
Oxendale	Ann	M		Hutton	
Oxendale	Peeter		6		
Oxendale	Alice		4	and	
Oxendale	Ann		2	Longton	
Osbeldeston	Isabella				
Orbin	Thos			Cr	
Osbeldeston	George			High St	
Osbeldeston	Ann				
Olchroft	Margret	M			
Olchroft	Patrick		13		
Olchroft	Willm		7		
Olchroft	Mary		5		
Ornns?	John				
Oalbin	Thos	F			
Oalbin	Margret	M			
Oalbin	Betty		x		
Oalbin	John		17		17
Oalbin	James		10		
Oalbin	Agness		7		
Oalbin	Robt		4		
Olbendestion	John	F			
Olbendestion	Ann	M			
Olbendestion	Bellow		13x		
Olbendestion	Betty		9		
Olbendestion	John		7		
Olbendestion	Joseph		4		
Olbendestion	Willm		3		
Olbendestion	James		1		
Pemberton	Richd				
Postlethwaith	Wm		14	John St	
	George		11		
Porter	Mary		18	Clarke Yd	
Patten	Margt		14	Church St	
	Nancy		11	Church St	
	Jane		17	John St	
Preston	Robert	F		St John St	
	Helen	M			
	Robert		17		
	John		15		
	Helen		17		
	Richd		11		
	Anne		15		18

1810 Census   Catholic Congregation of Preston

Surname	Forename(s)	Rel	Age	Address	Comm
Proctor	Mathew	F		Church St	
	Mary	M			
	Mary				
Paley	Mr P			Church St	
Paley	Mrs				
Park	James		22	L Water St	
Pemberton	Ellen	Sv			
	Mary				
Parkinson	Sarah				
Proctor	James	F		Mt St	
Proctor	Mary	M			
Proctor	William		22		
Proctor	Thos		20		
Proctor	Evan		16		
Proctor	Martha		11		
Proctor	Mary		9		
Parker	Ann				
Parker	Alice				
Proctor	Henry	F		Rib Lane	
Proctor	Betty	M			
Proctor	William		x		
Palmer	Ann			Ch St	
Patrick	John		49	Dke	
Patrick	Alice		42		
Porter	Jane		28	Dk St	
Parkinson	John	F			
Parkinson	Catherine	M			
Parkinson	Sarah		7		
Parkinson	Elling		5		
Parkinson	George		3		
Parkinson	Thomas		2		
Parkinson	William		1		
Pemberton	Edward	F			
Pemberton	Jane		8		
Pemberton	Catherine		6		
Pemberton	Ann		5		
Pemberton	Mary		2		
Proctor	John			Lune St	
Parkinson	Thos	F		Qn St	
	Ann	M			
	Thos		17		
	Margery		15		
Parkinson	Robt	F			
	Mary	M			
	Ann		5		
	Dorothy		2		
Parkinson	James				
	Sally				
Proctor	Betty	M			
Proctor	Betty		21x		

1810 Census   Catholic Congregation of Preston

Surname	Forename(s)	Rel	Age	Address	Comm
Proctor	Peggy		19x		
Proctor	Frances		15x		
Proctor	Richard		9		
Proctor	William		8		
Proctor	Paul		4		
Parkinson	Frank	F			
Parkinson	Ann	M			
Parkinson	William		15		
Parkinson	Frank		7		
Poding	James	F			
Poding	Alice	M			
Postlewhite	William		x	St John St	
Postlewhite	George		9		
Pharrol	Margret	M	x	Vicar St	
Pharrol	Patrick		16		
Parker	John		x		
Parker	Jane		x		
Park	Henry	F	x	Snow Hill	
Park	Margret	M			
Park	Betty		6		
Park	Richard		3		
Park	John		1		
Poulton	Betty		x		
Preston	Elling	M		St John St	
Preston	Robert		x		
Preston	John		x		
Preston	Elling		x		
Preston	Richard		12		
Preston	Ann		5		
Pemberton	Jonathan	F		Whittaker row	
Pemberton	Jane	M			
Pemberton	Jane		1		
Pemberton	James		24	Ld St	
Pemberton	Betty		1		
Parkinson	William		19	Wood St	
Parkinson	James	F	49	New H	
Parkinson	Elizabeth	M	49		
Parkinson	John		20		
Parkinson	Richard		14		
Parkinson	Mary		10		
Parkinson	James		8		
Parkinson	Ann		6		
Parkinson	Eliz		5		
Parkinson	Willm		3		
Pickup	Ann		40	Square	
Pickup	Betty		18		
Parrish	Margret		30		
Parkinson	Betty			Parradice St	
Procter	Ralph				
Procter	Alice				

1810 Census Catholic Congregation of Preston

Surname	Forename(s)	Rel	Age	Address	Comm
Procter	Ann	M		York St	
Procter	Mary				
Procter	Easter		20		
Park	Martin	F		Willow St	
Park	Ellen	M			
Park	James				
Park	John				
Park	Margret				
Park	Joseph				
Park	Mary				
Park	Thos				
Park	Robert				
Pool	William		60		
Pool	Margret		50		5
Parkinson	Betty		40		
Parkinson	Peggy		14		
Parkinson	Matty		11		
Parkinson	Nany		5		
Parkinson	Betty				
Parris	Jane			Holden square	
Parris	Ann		8		
Parkinson	Mary	Wd			
Parkinson	Catherine		12		
Preston	Widdow				
Preston	Sarah		21		
Parkinson	Bellow				
Parkinson	Elizth		9		
Parkinson	Jane		5		
Parkinson	Willm	F		Union St	
Parkinson	Ellen	M			
Parkinson	Ann		17		
Parkinson	John		15		
Parkinson	Robt		12		
Parkinson	Thos		8		
Parkinson	Stephen		5		
Parkinson	Jane		2		
Prescot	Elling	M		Frirg	
Prescot	John		10		
Prescot	Margret		6		
Prescot	Mary		2		
Parkinson	Willm	F		Bowling G	
Parkinson	Alice	M			
Parkinson	Mary		7		
Parkinson	Ann		5		
Parkinson	Thos		2		
Parkinson	Margret	M		Frier G	
Parkinson	Jane		17x		
Peart	Widdow				
Peart	Richd		18		
Peart	John		13		

1810 Census   Catholic Congregation of Preston

Surname	Forename(s)	Rel	Age	Address	Comm
Peart	Hanah		12		
Preston	Robt	Hu			
Preston	Ann	Wf			
Porter	Jane				
Pemberton	Richd				
Parker	Betty				
Proctor	John	F			
Proctor	Ann	M			
Proctor	John		13		
Proctor	Thos		11		
Proctor	Aice		5		
Proctor	Ralph		4		
Proctor	Molley		2		
Proctor	Margret				
Parker	Joseph		14x		
Parker	James	F			
Parker	Ann	M			
Parker	Richd		1		
Parker	Christopher		4		
Pope	Richd	F			
Pope	Margret	M			
Pope	Margery				
Pope	Ann		8		
Pope	Sarah		4		
Pope	Geo		3		
Pope	John		1		
Proctor	Ann				
Proctor	Geo				
Proctor	Robt				
Parkinson	Thos	F			
Parkinson	Jane	M			
Parkinson	Betty		8		
Parkinson	Betty		8		
Rigby	Anne	Wd		Church St	
	Anne		13		
	Richd		11		
	Mary		9		
	Joseph		7		
Roper	Anne		40	Church St	19
Richardson	Betty	Wd		Blue Bell Yd	
	William		6		
	Richd		1		
Raby	John			Mt St	
Raby	Martha				
Rodginson	Richd	Sv			1
Robertson	Mary	Sv			1
Roddice	Rosela	Sv			1
Ratcliff	Ann	Sv			1
Rawcliff	Betty	Sv			20
Rawcliff	Winifred	M			

1810 Census   Catholic Congregation of Preston

Surname	Forename(s)	Rel	Age	Address	Comm
Rawcliff	John		8		
Rawcliff	Ann		4		
Rawcliff	Catherine		1		
Rawcliffe	Ann				
Richardson	Margaret				
Roskell	Roger	F			
Roskell	Mary	M			
Roskell	Thomas		5		
Roskell	Robert		2		
Roskell	James		1		
Ribchester	John	F			
Ribchester	Jane	M			
Ribchester	John		12		
Ribchester	Sarah		10		
Robinson	Margaret	M			
Robinson	Ann		7		
Robinson	William		6		
Robinson	Betty		3		
Robinson	John		1		
Richardson	John	F			
	Betty	M			
	Agnes		6		
	Betty		5		
Robinson	Joseph	F			
Robinson	Betty	M			
Robinson	John		5		
Robinson	Mary		3		
Rowlinson	Ann		x	Snowhill	
Rowlinson	Jane		x		
Rowlinson	Thomas		1		
Rushton	William	F			
Rushton	Mary	M			
Rushton	Margret		3		
Rushton	Martha		2		
Rushton	James		1		
Ralph	Robert		19	Fable St	
Robbison	Mary		34		
Rainford	Alice	M	64		
Rainford	James		29	New St	
Roper	Robert	F	52	Lord St	
Roper	Lucy	M	50		
Roper	Eliz		24		
Roper	Ellen		20		
Roper	Mary		17		
Roper	Ann		15		
Roper	Lucy		11		
Roper	William		7		
Roper	Maria		5		
Robinson	Alice	Sv	18		
Riley	Peeter			Paradice St	

1810 Census   Catholic Congregation of Preston

Surname	Forename(s)	Rel	Age	Address	Comm
Riley	Hannah				
Riley	Margret				
Riley	Ellen				
Riley	William				
Rainford	Nic	F		Holden Square	
Rainford	John		13		
Rainford	Martin		12		
Rainford	Isabella		11		
Rainford	Mary		2		21
Rainford	Ann		7		
Rainford	Anthony		6		
Ratcliff	Charles	F		Heatley St	
Ratcliff	Margret	M			
Ratcliff	Mary		8		
Ratcliff	Ann		9		
Ratcliff	Thos		1		
Rigby	Rt	F			
Rigby	Richard		40		
Rigby	James		36		
Rigby	Robert		28		
Rigby	Alice		32		
Rogison	Widdow				
Roskell	Willm				
Roberts	Mary	M		frierg	
Roberts	Thos		4		
Roberts	Robt		1		
Rig	John	F			
Rig	Agness	M			
Rig	Jane		4		
Rig	Mary		1		
Rostron	Christopher				
Rostron	Jane				
Rostron	Joseph		20		
Rostron	Grandaughter	GD	6		
Richardson	John	F		Back Lane	
Richardson	Eliz	M			
Richardson	Margret		9		
Richardson	Elling		5		
Richardson	Willm		3		
Richardson	Alice		1		
Rigby	Thos		107	Sing	
Rigby	Catherine				
Row	Bridget		7		
Ribchester	Michal	F			
Ribchester	Ann	M			
Ribchester	John		20		
Ribchester	Ann		14		
Rigby	Mary			High St	
Rigby	Ellen		13x		
Rostrone	Betty				

1810 Census   Catholic Congregation of Preston

Surname	Forename(s)	Rel	Age	Address	Comm
Renals	Henry				
Rockliff	Ann				
Rockliff	Alice	M			
Rockliff	Alice		x		
Rockliff	Margt		x		
Rockliff	Ellen		x		
Sharrock	Peter			L Church St	
Simpson	James	F		Church St	22
	Mary	M			
	Helen		2		
Swarbrick	John	F		Rose St	
	Jane	M			
	George		22		
Sidgreaves	George			Church yd	
Shakeshaft	Law	F		Syke St	
	Mary	M			
	Richd		11		
	Ellis		8		
	Elizabeth		4		
	John		1		
Seed	Mary			John St	
Stephenson	Sarah			John St	23
Seed	Ellen		22		
Southworth	James			Church St	
	Judith	Wf			
Slater	George			Dale St	
Speddy	Joseph	F			
	Catherine	M			
	Wm		3		
	Sarah		1		
Smith	Hellen		19		
Simson	Margarat				
Slater	Margarat				
Southward	Margt	Sv			
Sharrock	Mary				
	Winey				
Smith	Sarah			Mt St	
Siddall	William				
Slater	Charles	F			
Slater	Betty	D	18		
Slater	Ellen		16		
Slater	Wm	S	15		
Slater	Charles		12		
Singleton	Ellen				
Smith	Mary				
Salsbury	Ann	M		Fishr G	
Salsbury	Agnes	D			
Stazziker	Nancy	M		Ch St	
Stazziker	William		4		
Stazziker	Mary		2		

1810 Census   Catholic Congregation of Preston

Surname	Forename(s)	Rel	Age	Address	Comm
Stazziker	Eliza		1		
Simpson	William	F			
Simpson	Betty	M			
Simpson	William		4		
Simpson	Richard		1		
Sumner	Rosy	M		Rib Lane	
Sumner	Ellin		6		
Smith	Thomas				
Stains	John				
Smith	James	F			
Smith	Mary	M			
Smith	Jane		10		
Smith	Thomas		7		
Smith	Richard		4		
Smith	Nancy		1		
Skillings	Patrick	F			
Skillings	James		3		
Snape	Thomas			Ch St	
Smith	William		38	Dk	
Smith	Mary		40		
Smith	Betty		12		
Smith	Jane		9		
Speakman	William	F			
Speakman	Mary	M			
Speakman	John		1		
Slater	Ann		47	Park L	
Slater	Ann		24	Th	
Sherrington	William				
Sherrington	Elizabeth				
Singleton	John	F			
Singleton	Ann	M			
Singleton	John		+		
Singleton	William		9		
Singleton	Richard		4		
Shakeshaft	Henry				
Shakeshaft	Mary				
Shakeshaft	Thomas	F			
Shakeshaft	Mary	M			
Shakeshaft	Henry		4		
Shakeshaft	Robert		3		
Shakeshaft	Thos		2		
Shakeshaft	John		1		
Smith	Henry	F			
Smith	Mary	M			
Smith	Jane		7		
Smith	James		5		
Smith	Henry		3		
Smith	George		1		
Seeds	Robert				
Seeds	Dorothy				

1810 Census   Catholic Congregation of Preston

Surname	Forename(s)	Rel	Age	Address	Comm
Seeds	Thomas				
Smith	Henry				
Southam	Ann				
Smith	James	F			
Smith	Ann	M			
Smith	Christopher				
Smith	John		28	Vauxhall Road	
	Alice		26		
	Grace		7		
	Richd		5		
	Elizth		3		
	Silvester		3m		24
Sheppard	Ellen	M			
Sheppard	Jane				
Shepard	Mary		2		
Stell	John	F			
Stell	Betty	M			
Stell	John		6		
Sagor	Adam	F			
Sagor	Nancy	M			
Sagor	John		22		
Sagor	Mary		14x		
Sagor	William		9		
Simpson	Thomas	F			
Simpson	Nancy	M			
Simpson	William		3		
Shannon	Martin	Hu			
Shannon	Betty	Wf			
Smith	Mary	M		Starchhouse	
Smith	Nancy		x		
Shephard	Thomas	F		Vicar St	
Shepard	Margret	M			
Shepard	Robert		6		
Shepard	Richard		5		
Shepard	James		3		
Shepard	Mary		1		
Shepard	Robert	F			
Shepard	Deborah	M			
Shepard	William		14		
Shepard	James		6		
Smith	Richard	F			
Smith	Nancy	M			
Smith	Margret		22		
Sherrington	Henry	F			
Sherrington	Elling	M			
Sherrington	William		6		
Sherrington	John		4		
Smith	Elling				
Seeds	Elling				
Southworth	James				

1810 Census Catholic Congregation of Preston

Surname	Forename(s)	Rel	Age	Address	Comm
Southworth	Judith				
Slaytor	Mary	M			
Slaytor	Nancy		3		
Simpson	Michael			Whittaker Row	
Simpson	Betty				
Syddal	George	F			
Syddal	Grace	M			
Syddal	Mary		13		
Syddal	Margret		10		
Syddal	John		7		
Syddal	Nancy		4		
Syddal	Joseph		2		
Slaytor	Catherine				
Swarbrick	Ellen		26	Back L	
Shakeshaft	Law	F	40	New St	
Shakeshaft	Ann	M	40		
Shakeshaft	Thomas		10		
Shakeshaft	Ann		9		
Shakeshaft	Sarah		7		
Shakeshaft	Grace		5		
Shakeshaft	Alic		1		
Smith	Margret	Sv	24		
Siddle	Alice	Sv	16		
Seed	Ann		17	Wood St	
Smith	Mary		57		
Smith	John	F			
Smith	Ellen	M			
Smith	Thos		13		
Smith	Catherine		9		
Slinger	Richard				
Swinlest	Betty		15	York St	
Swinlest	Willm		13		
Swinlest	Ann		6		
Swinles	John		17		
Shakeshaft	Mr		33		
Shakeshaft	Mrs		33		25
Stringfellow	William		26		
Stringfellow	Ann		26		
Singleton	Thos		56		
Singleton	Mary		58		
Singleton	Willm		21		
Singleton	Joseph		18		
Singleton	Mary		19		
Singleton	Peggy		11		
Sherrington	James			Dale St	
Sherrington	Emry				
Sherrington	Thos		4		
Sherrington	John		10		
Sherrington	Mary		1		
Smith	Alice				

1810 Census   Catholic Congregation of Preston

Surname	Forename(s)	Rel	Age	Address	Comm
Smith	Mary		9		
Slater	John				26
Slater	Thos	F			
Slater	Ellen	M			
Slater	Ann		23		
Slater	Margt		21		
Slater	Susan		17		
Slater	William		12		
Slater	John		9		
Slater	Mary		6		
Slater	Joseph		4		
Salts	Mary				
Salts	Jane		6		
Salts	Rich		9		
Slater	Mary	M		Dale St	
Slater	Ellen		9		
	Alice		5		
Sherrington	Edward	F		Holden Square	
Sherrington	Jane	M			
Sherrington	Betty		23		
Sherrington	Ellen		18		
Sherrington	Edward		11		
Sherrington	Willm		6		
Spencer	Ann				
Smith	Alice				
Smith	Mary		9		
Smith	James		3		
Southward	John			Dale St	
Slater	Saragh				
Salts	Jane				
Shakeshaft	John			Stanley St	
Shakeshaft	Sarah				
Shakeshaft	Sarah		29		
Shakeshaft	William		22		
Sheels	Hugh		x		
Smith	Mary		x		
Stockley	Widdow			Heatley St	
Stockley	Mary		11		
Stockley	John		10		
Seed	John	F			
Seed	Ann	M			
Seed	Thos		2		
Seed	John				
Simmons	Widdow				
Simmons	Mary		18		
Slater	Widdow				
Slater	Ann		33		
Slaytor	Jane		30		
Slaytor	Thos		28		
Spencer	John	F			

1810 Census — Catholic Congregation of Preston

Surname	Forename(s)	Rel	Age	Address	Comm
Spencer	Margret	M			
Spencer	Joseph		17		
Spencer	Dannial		12		
Spencer	Ann		10		
Spencer	Mary		8		
Spencer	John		3		
Spencer	Bridget		1		
Sharrock	Mary				
Sharrock	Winnifread				
Stevenson	John	F			
Stevenson	Mary	M			
Stevenson	Willm		17		
Stevenson	Jane		11		
Stevenson	Lawrance		9		
Stevenson	Elizth		1		
Smith	Thos	F			
Smith	Elizth	M			
Smith	Elizth		29		
Smith	Mary		23		
Smith	Agness		18		
Shakeshaft	Betty			Sing	
Salthouse	Mary				
Smith	Richd	F			
Smith	Ann	M			
Smith	Ellen		14		
Smith	Margt		12		
Smith	Willm		9		
Smith	John		6		
Smith	Ann		4		
Smith	Richd		1		
Sidgreaves	Betty		15		
Sidgreaves	Mary		9		
Smith	James	F			
Smith	Jane	M			
Smith	Mary		3		
Smith	Betty		2		
Slator	Geo	F			
Slator	Mary	M			
Slator	Willm		12		
Slator	Betty		11		
Slator	Ann		8		
Slator	Jane		6		
Slator	James		4		
Slator	Mary		1		
Slator	John	F			
Slator	Betty	M			
Smith	John	F			
Smith	Elizth	M			
Smith	Mary		8		
Smith	Richd	F			

1810 Census   Catholic Congregation of Preston

Surname	Forename(s)	Rel	Age	Address	Comm
Smith	Nancy	M			
Smith	Thos		6		
Smith	Mary		4		
Smith	Jinney		3		
Smith	Alice		1		
Sharrock	Ralph	F			
Sharrock	Jane	M			
Sharrock	Willm		21		
Sharrock	Betty		16		
Sharrock	Ellen		9		
Sharrock	John		5		
Shepard	Margret	M			
Shepard	Willm		6		
Shepard	Nancy		3		
Sumner	Robt	F			
Sumner	Betty	M			
Sumner	Thos		2		
Sumner	Jane		3w		
Slator	Mary	M			
Slator	Richd		19		
Slator	Robt		10		
Slator	Margret		7		
Slator	Ann		18		
Simpson	Thos	F			
Simpson	Ann	M			
Simpson	Willm		3		
Simpson	Betty		1		
Smith	John	F			
Smith	Ann	M			
Smith	Thos		19		
Smith	Willm		17		
Smith	Robt		15		
Smith	Jane		13		
Smith	John		11		
Smith	Mary		9		
Smith	Alice		7		
Smith	Rachel		4		
Smith	Joseph		1		
Stankey	Betty				
Stankey	Barnley		4		
Sherlocker	Ellen	M			
Sherlocker	Nancy		x		
Simpson	James	F			
Simpson	Ann	M			
Simpson	Ann		5		
Simpson	Joseph		1		
Sanderson	Nicholas	F			
Sanderson	Frances	M			
Sanderson	Mary		1		
Shepard	Sarah				

1810 Census — Catholic Congregation of Preston

Surname	Forename(s)	Rel	Age	Address	Comm
Slator	Mary				
Snape	James				
Snape	Alice				
Smith	Thos	F			
Smith	Mart	M			
Smith	John		18		
Smith	Ann		11		
Sherliker	Ellen	M			
Sherliker	Betty		18x		
Sherliker	Ellen		13		
Sherliker	Mary		11		
Smith	James	F			
Smith	Margt	M			
Smith	Willm		22x		
Smith	Mary		21x		
Smith	John		19x		
Smith	Ann		14x		
Smith	Betty		12		
Smith	Margt		9		
Smith	Jane		7		
Smith	James		5		
Smith	Barnaby	F			
Smith	Ellin	M			
Smith	Alice		x		
Smith	Margery		x		
Smith	John		18		
Sherliker	Hannah		8		
Sherliker	John		5		
Savage	Ann				
Sherliker	Thos	F			
Sherliker	Ellen	M			
Sherliker	Joseph		8		
Sherliker	John		6		
Sherliker	Thos		4		
Sherliker	Robt		1		
Smith	Willm	F			
Smith	Nancy	M			
Smith	Sarah		9		
Smith	Mary		6		
Smith	Willm		4		
Smith	Nancy		1		
Shepard	Betty	M			
Shepard	Elling		x		
Shepard	Mary		6		
Shepard	Richd	F			
Shepard	Jane	M			
Shepard	Jane		2		
Slator	John	F			
Slator	Bellow	M			
Slator	Willm		3		

1810 Census — Catholic Congregation of Preston

Surname	Forename(s)	Rel	Age	Address	Comm
Slator	Mary		1		
Taberner	Henry	F		Sch St	
	Elizabeth	M			
	Joseph		7		
	Alice		4		
Tipping	Thomas	F		Cch St	
	Jane	M			
	Richard		13		
	William		11		
	Nancy		9		
	Annah		7		
	Mary		4		
	Thomas		1		
Talbot	John			Cch St	
Townsend	Isabel			Cch St	
Thompson	Margaret	Wd			
	John		11		
	Mary Ann		3		
Turner	George	F		Ch St	
	Elizabeth	M			
	Ann		17		
	John		16		
	Thomas		15		
	William		11		27
Talbot	William	F			27
	Catherine	M			
	Dorothy		9		
	Elizabeth		5		
	Catherine		3		
Turner	Thomas	F		Mt St	
Turner	Ann	M			
Turner	Mary		6		
Turner	Ann		3		
Towers	Betty				
Topping	William		0	Crn	
Tomlinson	Sarah				
Twist	John	F	45	Dk	
Twist	Ann	M	40		
Twist	John		14		
Twist	William		12		
Twist	Michael		9		
Twist	Peter		8		
Twist	James		6		
Twist	George		3		
Townson	Mary		x		
Tootel	Winifred				
Towers	John				
	Ellin				
Townley	Margret	M			
Townley	Richard		12		

1810 Census   Catholic Congregation of Preston

Surname	Forename(s)	Rel	Age	Address	Comm
Townley	Charles		8		
Taylor	James				26
Turner	Betty		52	Hutton	
Travis	Thomas	F		and	
Travis	John		4	Longton	
Taylor	James	F	58		
Taylor	Betty	M	64		
Taylor	Peeter		26		
Talbot	William	F	78	Lord St	
Tabot	Dorothy	M	76		
Tabot	Ellen		40		
Teeby	Catherine	M	38		
Teeby	George	F	40		
Teeby	Robert		2		
Teeby	James		1		
Tyby	J	Hu	28	Shambles	
Tyby	Ellen	Wf	32		
Taylor	Mary			Leeming St	
	Eliza		6		
Talbot	Margret			Parradice St	
Taylor	Widdow	M			
Taylor	Ann		9		
Taylor	John		5		
Taylor	Margret		2		
Thornton	Lucy			Friargate	
Taylor	John	F			
Taylor	Mary	M			
Taylor	Elizth		18x		
Taylor	Mary		15x		
Taylor	Agness		12		
Taylor	Jane		10		
Taylor	John		8		
Taylor	Joseph		5		
Taylor	Elling		4		
Taylor	Ann		2		
Taylor	Thos		1		
Taylor	Geo	F			
Taylor	Ann Walsh		40		
	Margret		12		28
Taylor	Margery		10		
Taylor	George		1		
Townsend	James	F			
Townsend	Jane	M			
Townsend	Charles		15		
Townsend	Benedict		13		
Townsend	James		11		
Townsend	Joseph		10		
Townsend	Richd		7		
Townsend	Mary		4		
Townsend	Margret		2		

1810 Census — Catholic Congregation of Preston

Surname	Forename(s)	Rel	Age	Address	Comm
Thornton	Widdow			friergate	
Thornton	Margret		10		
Thornton	John		8		
Thornton	James		3		
Taylor	George			High St	
Tomlinson	Hanah				
Tempest	Ann				
Tootell	James	F			
Tootell	Jane	M			
Tootell	Thos		8		
Tootell	Mary		7		
Tootell	Mark		5		
Tootell	John		3		
Tootell	Sarah		1		
Taylor	John	F		More Lane	
Taylor	Mary	M			
Taylor	Alice		13		
Taylor	James		11		
Taylor	Betty		9		
Taylor	William		5		
Taylor	Mary		1		
Valentine	Alice			Mt St	
Vose	John	Hu	28	Back Lane	
Vose	Ann	Wf	29		
Valentine	Richard	Hu	22	New St	
Valentine	Betty	Wf	22		
Vose	John			Holden Square	
Vose	Mary				
Vose	Betty		6		
Vose	Thos				
Vose	Mary				
Vose	John				
Valentine	James			High St	
Valentine	Mary				
Valentine	Margret		2		
Wallis	Ann	Wd		Old Dog Yd	
	Henry		15		
	Nancy		23		
	Jenny		12		
Wilding	Mary	Wd		Clk Yd	
	James		3		
	Thomas		6		
Woodacre	William	F		Jno St	
	Jane	M			
	Ellen		24		
Wilson	Thomas	F		Jno St	
	Ellen	M			
	Peter		5		
Wrigley	Betty		24	Cch St	
Wilson	Benn	F		Blue Bell Yd	

1810 Census　　　　　　　　Catholic Congregation of Preston

Surname	Forename(s)	Rel	Age	Address	Comm
[Wilson]	Agness	M			
	Henry		13		
	James		11		
	John		6		
	Richd		2		
Windle	Chas			Cch Gates	
Wilding	Elizabeth				
Wilcock	John				
	Ellen				
Wren	Mary				
	Thomas				
Woodcock	Elizabeth	M			
	Jane				
	Mary				
Wilson	George	F			
	Alice	M			
	William		3		
	Mary		1		
Whittam	James				
	Richard				
Wilcock	James	F		Mt St	
Wilcock	Mary	M			
Wilcock	John		5		
Wilcock	Jane		3		
Wilcock	Margaret		1		
Woodcock	Jenny	M		Mt St	
Woodcock	Betty	D	1		
Woodcock	Mary				
Woodcock	Thos			Fish G	
Woodcock	William				
Wilcock	Sally			Sing	
Whalley	Robt	F			
Whalley	Ann	M			
Whalley	Joseph	S	1m		
Whittle	James	F			
Whittle	Jenney	M			
Whittle	Sally		10		
Whittle	Betty		8		
Whittle	Henry		5		
Whittle	Jenny		3		
Whittle	Joseph		6w		
Whittle	Mary		6w		
Waterhouse	Richd	F			
Waterhouse	Molly	M			
Waterhouse	Betty		6		
Walmsley	Giles			Sing	
Wearden	Ann	M			
Wearden	Jenny		9		
Wearden	Ann		5m		
Whittle	William	F			

1810 Census   Catholic Congregation of Preston

Surname	Forename(s)	Rel	Age	Address	Comm
Whittle	Winny	M			
Whittle	Margaret		27		
Whittle	William		5		
Whittle	John		3		
Woodcock	George	F		Sing	
Woodcock	Ellen	M			
Woodcock	Mary Ann		3		
Woodcock	Jane		1		
Woodcock	John	F			
Woodcock	Betty	M			
Woodcock	Bellow		8		
Woodcock	James		6		
Woodcock	Nancy		3		
Woodcock	Thomas		2		
Woodcock	Richard		7w		
Wearden	Dolly			Sing	
Woodcock	Thos	F			
Woodcock	Ellen	M			
Woodcock	Mary		4		
Woodcock	Roger		18m		29
Wiggins	Thomas			Crook	
Wilding	Joseph	F		Crn	
Wilding	Betty	M			
Wilding	George		5		
Wilding	Thomas		3		
Wilding	Robert		1		
Whalley	William	F		Crn	
Whalley	Betty	M			
Whalley	William		16		
Whalley	John		1		
Wilcock	James			Crn	
Wilcock	Peggy				
Watson	Jane	Sv			1
Wilson	Mrs		60		
Wareing	George		4		
Wareing	George		35		
Wareing	Peggy		40		
Wilson	Thos		3		
Wilson	Ann		2		
Ward	Joseph		31	Ch lne	
Ward	Peggy		31		
Ward	William		10		
Ward	Richd		7		
Ward	Margaret		5		
Ward	John		3		
Woodcock	James	F	60	Kg St	
Woodcock	Ann	M	55		
Woodcock	Molly		15		
Woodcock	Nanny		13		
Whittle	George	F	45	Kg St	

1810 Census   Catholic Congregation of Preston

Surname	Forename(s)	Rel	Age	Address	Comm
Whittle	Molly	M	47		
Whittle	Ellin		24		
Whittle	Diana		20		
Whittle	Mary		18		
Whittle	Peggy		15		
Whiteside	George	F	40	B 1770	
Whiteside	Bellow	M	38		
Whiteside	Betty		12		
Whiteside	Kitty		10		
Whiteside	Margaret		7		
Whiteside	Mary		6		
Whiteside	Jane		3		
Whiteside	George		1		
Whitehead	Jane		14		
Wilcock	Margaret		1		
Walker	Alice		x	Blk H Yard	
Walker	Thos				
Walker	Mary				
Walmsley	William				
Worden	Mary		20	Walton St	
Willacy	James	Wr			
Willacy	-		15		
Whittle	Mary		87	Vauxh Road	
Woodroof	Henry		27		
	Margaret		37		
	James		3		
	Betty		10		
Woodcock	Thos		26		
	Mary		26		
	Fanny		7		
	Betty		6		
	Margt		2		
Winder	Jane		0		
Whittle	John		0		
Waterhouse	Betty	M			
Waterhouse	James				
Waterhouse	Hew				
Waterhouse	Charles				
Waterhouse	James	F			
Waterhouse	Betty	M			
Waterhouse	Alice		4		
Waterhouse	Mary		1		
Waterhouse	John	F			
Waterhouse	Nancy	M			
Waterhouse	James		19		
Waterhouse	John		15x		
Waterhouse	Betty		12		
Waterhouse	Thomas		10		
Waterhouse	Kitty		4		
Walton	John	F			

1810 Census　　Catholic Congregation of Preston

Surname	Forename(s)	Rel	Age	Address	Comm
Walton	Martin	M			
Walton	Ann		8		
Walton	Thomas		6		
Woodruff	Henry		4		
Wilding	Thomas	F			
Wilding	Jane	M			
Wilding	Nancy		12		
Waring	Richard	F			
Waring	Mary	M			
Waring	John		16		
Waring	Rodger		11		
Wilkinson	Henry	F			
Wilkinson	Catherine		18		
Wilkinson	Henry		16		
Wilkinson	Hannah		14		
Wilkinson	Thomas		9		
Walton	Richard	F		Vicar St	
Walton	Agness	M			
Walton	Betty		4		
Walton	Mary		6		
Walton	Dorothy		2		
Walton	Peeter		1		
Willson	James	F			
Willson	Esther	M			
Willson	Margret		17		
Willson	Betty		14		
Willson	Anges		12		
Willson	John		9		
Willson	Mary		7		
Willson	Nancy		5		
Warbrick	Robert	F		Snow hill	
Warbrick	Joseph		x		
Warbrick	Janes		9		
Wiggins	Thomas	F	x	Back lane	
Wiggins	James		x		
Wiggins	Jane		x		
Wiggins	Nancy		x		
Walmsley	Mary			Tythe Barn St	
Walmsley	Ann	M			
Walmsley	Mary		x		
Walmsley	Ralph		13		
Whaly	Ann	M			
Whaly	Thomas		x		
Wilcock	Christopher	F		St John St	
Wilcock	Elling	M			
Wilcock	Jane		5		
Wilcock	Margret		3		
Wilcock	Betty		2		
Wilcock	Alice		1		
Waddaker	William	F			

1810 Census — Catholic Congregation of Preston

Surname	Forename(s)	Rel	Age	Address	Comm
Waddaker	Jane	M			
Waddaker	Elling		x		
Wilding	Mary	M		Clark yard	
Wilding	Thomas		6		
Wilding	James		3		
Whittle	Betty			Whittaker Row	
Wobank	Ann	M		Hutton	
Wobank	Jane		6		
Wobank	Ralph		3		
Woodcock	George		21	and	
Worsley	Betty	M			
Worsley	George		11		
Worsley	Betty		1	Longton	
Wearden	George	F	58	Back Lane	
Wearden	Ellen	M	40		
Wearden	Robert		10		
Wearden	John		4		
Wilkinson	James	Hu	24		
Wilkinson	Sarah	Wf	24		
Wyke	William	F	27	Shambles	
Wyke	Esther	M	27		
Wyke	Elizabeth		13		
Wyke	Esther		5		
Wyke	Ann		1		
Winstanly	Alice	Sv	30		
Whittle	Mary			Leeming St	
Whittle	Margret				
Whard	Henry				
Walmsley	Jane	M		Parradice St	
Walmsley	Betty				
Walmsley	Ellen				
Walmsley	Ann		7		
Walmsley	Jane				
Worthington	Thos	F			
Worthington	Jane	M			
Worthington	Richard		19		
Worthington	John		18		
Worthington	James		15		
Worthington	Mathew		9		
Worthington	Jane		12		
Worthington	Winnd?		11		
Walmsley	Ann			Holden Square	
Wesbeter	Mary		29		
Willson	Mary	M			
Willson	Sarah		14		
Willson	Alice		12		
Willson	William		11		
Willson	Edward		10		
Walmsley	William		x		
Walmsley	Ann		x		

1810 Census   Catholic Congregation of Preston

Surname	Forename(s)	Rel	Age	Address	Comm
Walmsley	William			Stanley St	
Wilacy	James	F		Dale St	
Wilacy	Mary	M			
Wilacy	John		16		
Wilacy	Henry		4		
Wilacy	Alice		12		
Willacy	James		6		
Wilacy	Mary		10		
Wilacy	Ann		1		
Wareing	John				
Wareing	Mary				
Wareing	Rachel		19		
Wareing	John		12		
Walmsley	James			Dale St	
Walmsley	Agness				
Walton	James			Heatley St	
Walton	Mary	Sl			
Walker	John	F			
Walker	Jane	M			
Walmsley	James	F		Briget St	
Walmsley	Elling	M			
Walmsley	John		27		
Walmsley	Margret		24		
Walmsley	Thos		21		
Walmsley	James		18		
Walmsley	Willm		12		
Walmsley	Mary		7		
Walmsley	Elling		5		
Woodroof	Thos				
Widgan	Ann	M			
Widgan	Margret		25		
Widgan	Ann		19		
Widgan	Cathrine		17		
Widgan	Grace		10		
Willcock	James		7		
Williams	Ellen			Frierg	
Williams	Isabella		21		
Williams	Willm		16		
Williams	Elizabeth		10		
	Richard				30
Wiggans	Thos	F			
Wigans	Ann		17		
Wigan	James		16		
Wigan	Jane		14		
Woodruff	Thos			Frierg	
Woodruff	Margret				
Wareing	Thos	F			
Wareing	Elizth	M			
Wareing	Joseph		15		
Wareing	Ann		12		

1810 Census   Catholic Congregation of Preston

Surname	Forename(s)	Rel	Age	Address	Comm
Wareing	Mary		9		
Wareing	Ruth		7		
Wareing	Elizth		5		
Wareing	Thos				
Wadson	John	F			
Wadson	Jane	M			
Wadson	Margret		19		
Wadson	Ann		17		
Woodruff	Charles	F			
Woodruff	Ann	M			
Woodruff	Mary		29		
Willcock	Danl	F		Lils Yd	
Willcock	Charles		14		
Walsh	Lawrance		20	Frierg	
Wilson	Sarah			Back Lane	
Walmsley	Thos		15		
Walmsley	Richd				
Woods	Peeter	F			
Woods	Martha	M			
Woods	Edward		19x		
Woods	Margret		18		
Woods	Martha		14		
Woods	Mary		11		
Woods	Martha		3		
Whittle	Henry	F			
Whittle	Jane	M			
Whittle	Alice		4		
Whittle	Winfred		1		
Wareing	Betty				
Wareing	Ellen				
Wrocliff	Sarah	M			
Wrocliff	Robt		18x		
Wrocliff	Joseph		15		
Wrocliff	Thos		13		
Wrocliff	Ann		10		
Wrocliff	Geo		5		
Walker	Thos				
Walker	Margt				
Watson	Henry				
Watson	Ann				
Walker	Thos				
Walker	Ann				
Walton	Thos	GF			
Walton	Mary	GM			
Edmindson	Mary				
Wilkinson	James			Everton G	
Wilkinson	Geo				
Wilcock	John				
Ward	Margt			High St	
Ward	Mary		14		

1810 Census   Catholic Congregation of Preston

Surname	Forename(s)	Rel	Age	Address	Comm
Ward	Timothy		11		
Ward	John		9		
Ward	Thos		6		
Ward	Alice		3		
Wareing	Thos				
Wareing	Mary				
Woodruff	Thos		12		
Waterhouse	Thos	F			
Waterhouse	Ann	M			
Waterhouse	Able		15x		
Waterhouse	Mary		12		
Waterhouse	Betty		10		
Waterhouse	Willm		8		
Waterhouse	Ann		7		
Waterhouse	Thos		5		
Waterhouse	Charles		3		
Waterhouse	Jane		1		
Whaley	Mary	M			
Whaley	Ann		14		
Whaley	Catherine		12		
Whaley	Jane		9		
Woods	Thos	F			
Woods	Betty	M			
Woods	Sarah		1		
Woods	Mary				
Welsh	James	F			
Welsh	Mary	M			
Welsh	John		x		
Welsh	Margery		x		
Welsh	Joseph		x		
Welsh	Betty		x		
Welsh	Winnifred		x		
Welsh	Alfred		11		
Wilcock	William	F			
Wilcock	Betty	M			
Wilcock	Treasa		21x		
Wilcock	Margret		15x		
Wilcock	Mary		10		
Wilcock	Agness		7		
Wilcock	James		5		
Wilcock	William		1		
Whittle	Robt	F		High St	
Whittle	Alice		23		
Whittle	Margret		x		
Whittle	Ann		x		
Whittle	Thos		x		
Whittle	Mary		9		
Willden	William				
Willden	Tomisson				
Warbrick	Joseph		19		

1810 Census　　　　　　　Catholic Congregation of Preston

Surname	Forename(s)	Rel	Age	Address	Comm
Woodacker	Betty	M			
Woodacker	Willm		20x		
Woodacker	Mary		16		
Walmsley	John	F			
Walmsley	Alice	M			
Walmsley	Joseph		1		31
Walmsley	Mary		1		31
Wareing	John	F			
Wareing	Betty	M			
Wareing	Willm		8		
Wareing	Thos		7		
Wareing	Rossamond		6		
Wareing	John		1		
Walmsley	Richard	F			
Walmsley	Margt	M			
Walmsley	Jane		1		
Wilding	Thos			Ribleton Lane	
Wareing	John	F			
Wareing	Betty	M			
Wareing	Betty		24		
Wareing	Ann		21		
Wareing	James		19		
Wareing	John		18		
Wareing	Agness		14		
Waring	Thos		9		
Waring	Henry		5		
Yates	Betty	M		Cch St	
	George		21		
	Agness		20		
	Anne		23		32

Arrowsmith Ellen — Cpl St.
Ainsworth John W Sq.
Atherton Richard 80
Atkinson Alice M. Fshg
Atkinson Mary D — 25
Atkinson Jas. F.
Anderson Nancy M.
Anderson Wm L. 6
Anderson Rich'd 3
Appleton Mary, Sprig.
Abbot Will. Cnl St.
Adamson John 9
Adamson Agnes M.
Adamson Rich'd 13
Adamson Jane 10
Adamson Mary 7
Adamson Eliz. 4
Adamson John 1
Adams Betty Dch L.
Anderson Hannah M. Beh L
Anderson W T. 7

Example of 1810 entries

1820 Census — Catholic Congregation of Preston

Surname	Forename(s)	Age	Address	Comm
Atkinson	Thomas	30	Park	
	Ann	30	"	
	Richard	7	"	
	William	4	"	
	Ellen	1	"	
Atkinson	Thomas	15	22 Nile St	
Atkinson	Alice	66	28 Fishergate	
	James	28	"	
Anderson	Nancy		46 "	
	William	17	"	
Arrowsmith	Mary	20	58 "	
Adamson	Sarah		West End	
Anderton	Richard	26	32 Mount	
	Richard	11	"	
Ashurst	Robert	22	2 Chapel	
Appleton	Joseph	45	113 Fishergate	
	Helen	48	"	
	Thomas	20	"	
	Ann	19	"	
	Catherine	17	"	
	James	13	"	
	Clare	11	"	
	Margaret	9	"	
	Elizabeth	8	"	
Atkinson	Richard	29	16 Ratcliff	
	Alice	24	"	
	John	4	"	
	Mary	2	"	
	Ellen	1	"	
Alston	Mary		Back Swainson Factory	
	Alice	17	"	
	John	9	"	
Astley	James		18 Duke	
	Margt		"	
	Margt	12	"	
	William	10	"	
	Betty	8	"	
	Mary	3	"	
	Eliza	1	"	
Astley	Edward		Top of Duke	
	John		"	
	Edward	16	"	
	Winifred		"	
Aikin	Thomas		33 "	
	Margt		"	
	Margt	14	"	
	John	21	"	
	Thomas	11	"	
Anderton	William		12 King St	
Abbott	John		Frenchwood	

1820 Census   Catholic Congregation of Preston

Surname	Forename(s)	Age	Address	Comm
[Abbott]	Sarah		[Frenchwood]	
	Margt		"	
	Jane		"	
	Martha		"	
Acres	John	26	King	
	Alice		"	
	James	8	"	
	William	6	"	
	Ellen	4	"	
	Hugh	2	"	
Akers	P-Henry	44	Singleton	
	Betty		"	
	Thomas	10	"	
	Alice	4	"	
	Mary	2	"	
Akers	Richard	28	"	
	Catherine		"	
Anderton	Mary		1 Craggs row	
	Betty	15	"	
	Joseph	5	"	
	James	3	"	
	Richard	1	"	
Ainsworth	John		Moore Lane	
	Martha		"	
	Ann	5	"	
	Thomas	3	"	
	Edward	1	"	
Ainsworth	John		Crown St	
	Martha		"	
	Ann	5	"	
	Thomas	3	"	
	Edward	1	"	
Anderton	Mary		Craggs	
	John		"	
Atkinson	John	75	7 Ribbleton Lane	
	Dorothy	66	"	
	Laws	21	"	
Armriding	James	56	Moorside	
	Mary	5-	"	
	Agnes	24	"	
	Maria	13	"	
Atkinson	Jonas	32	5 Stanley	
	Ann	32	"	
	Mary	5	"	
	John	3	"	
	William	1	"	
Acre	Ann	22	Ferneth	
Abbot	William	50	8 Canal Street	
	Jane	37	"	
	William	9	"	

1820 Census — Catholic Congregation of Preston

Surname	Forename(s)	Age	Address	Comm
[Abbot]	Mary	7	[Church Street]	
	Alice	5	"	
	Peter	3	"	
	Margt	1	"	
Anderson	Francis	80	15 Hope	
	Mary	80	"	
Abraham	William	58	35 Bridge	
	Joseph	15	"	
Arnson	Thomas	81	14 "	
Acre	Thomas	31	16 Bridge St Lane	
	Mary	42	"	
Atkinson	Betty	46	Bk Canal St	
	Edward	14	"	
	Betty	7	"	
	Ann	3	"	
Anderton	Margt	23	28 Vicar	
	William	1	"	
Alston	Maria		Friday St	
	Margaret	8	"	
	Catherine	6	"	
	Joseph	4	"	
	Ann	3	"	
	Thomas		"	
Alderness	Mary	58	10 New Street	
Accors	Peter	59	11 Hardmans Yard	
	Agnes	62	"	
	Catherine	29	"	
Arrowsmith	Richard	38	42 M'ket Place	
	Mary	36	"	
	Jane	13	"	
	Richard	9	"	
	John	7	"	
	Robert	5	"	
	George	3	"	
	Nicholas	2	"	
	Eliza	8	"	
Alexander	Wm	27	27 Friargate	
	Emma	40	"	
	William	1	"	
	James	13	"	
Ainsworth	John		Lune Street	
	Nancy		"	
	Elizabeth	7	"	
	Jane	5	"	
	Mary Ann	1	"	
Ashton	A	14	164 Friargate	
Abraham	Mary	55	167 "	
Alornd	Dorothy	43	176 "	
	Cuthbert	18	"	
Arkwright	Robert		Cock Yard	

79

1820 Census   Catholic Congregation of Preston

Surname	Forename(s)	Age	Address	Comm
[Arkwright]	Peggy		[Cock Yard]	
	Betsy	5	"	
	Mary	3	"	
Aslem	Mary		Library	
Allunda	James	33	35 High Street	
	Ann	38	"	
	Joseph	10	"	
	Jane	8	"	
	Betty	5	"	
Alston	John	36	52 "	
	Mary	34	"	
	Mary Ann	8	"	
	William	5	"	
	A--	4	"	
	Catherine	1	"	
Atkinson	Mary	38	96 "	
	Thomas	12	"	
Agpdenwall	Jane	53	11 Buxtons Yard	
Awthornwait	Catherine	37	5 Fable Street	
Allan	Richard	20	9 Snowhill	
	Elizabeth	18	"	
Anderson	Ann	34	Vicar	
	William	16	"	
	Edward	14	"	
	Richard	10	"	
	John	8	"	
	Mary	5	"	
Ashton	James	43	Vicar St	
	Betty	39	"	
	Helen	15	"	
	Catherine	17	"	
	Betty	12	"	
	John	7	"	
	Richard	1	"	
Anderton	John	34	Cheanhouses in Marshend	
	Mary	24	"	
Almond	Ellen		Fulwood	
Baldwin	William	33	11 St John St	
	Agnes	37	"	
	Agnes	13	"	
	Mary	12	"	
	Betsy	10	"	
	Alice	5	"	
	Ann	4	"	
	Ellen	2	"	
Billington	Mary	19	Park	
Booth	Margeret	44	"	
	Mary	17	"	
	John	13	"	
	Elizabeth	7	"	

1820 Census — Catholic Congregation of Preston

Surname	Forename(s)	Age	Address	Comm
[Booth]	Thomas	4	[Park]	
Billington	Rosana	16	"	
Bamber	Hugh	40	13 Spring Gardens	
	Ellen	47	"	
	Thomas	7	"	
	Mary	5		
Bald	William	42	Germans Yard	
	Ellen	35	"	
	Ann	9		
Banks	William	4	12 Holden Yard	
Banks	William	19	105 Church	
Banes	Jane	22	23 "	
Bran	Hannah	54	Dixons Yard	
	John	22	"	
	Mary	15	"	
Baldwin	Jesse	27	7 Church	
	Eliza	30	"	
	Mary Ann	5	"	
	Thomas	3	"	
	Eliza	1	"	
Barrow	John	42	6 Cock Yard	
Banks	Richard	37	11 Cock Yard	
	Betty	37	"	
	Nancy	21	"	
	Margeret	18	"	
	Mary	9	"	
	Thomas	5	"	
	John	2	"	
Blundell	Mary	11	6 Woodcocks Yard	
Burgus	Thomas	27	3 Butlers Court	
Blanchard	Jas		35 Fishergate	
	Ann	40	"	
Bains	Margeret	24		
Brown	Margeret	28	4 Willow Place	
Burkett	James	38	2 "	
Bowden	Agnes	14	57 Fishergate	
Bushell	Joseph		69 "	
	Lucy		"	
Bullen	Thomas	20	"	
Bamber	Margeret	48	"	
Bains	Margeret	24	10 St Wilfrid	
Bamber	Catherine	30	1 Lune	
Billington	Ellen	82	22 Mount	
Bradley	William		16 Cannon Street	
	Mary		"	
	Elizabeth		"	
Burkett	Agnes		Charles Street	
Billington	James	49	39 Mount	
Banks	Thomas	35	40 "	
	Elizabeth	15	"	

1820 Census　　　　　Catholic Congregation of Preston

Surname	Forename(s)	Age	Address	Comm
Baxter	Stephen	56	38 [Mount]	
	Jane	53	"	
	John	28	"	
	Mary	23	"	
Banks	Philip	37	"	
	Margeret		"	
	Philip Jun		"	
	Margeret		"	
	Philip Jun Jun		"	
Bonny	James	25	38 "	
Banks	Henry	25	17 "	
Batersby	James	32	"	
	Margeret	32	"	
	Thomas	4	"	
Bains	John	73	5 "	
Bell	Ruth	41	Chapel Walk Fishergate	
Bolland	Martha	23	17 Fishergate	
Bilsborrow	Elizabeth	20	3 Well	
	Thomas	59	"	
	Alice	49	"	
	Richard	18	"	
	Ann	15	"	
Brindle	Christopher	30	4 Boram	
	William	5	"	
	Ellen	2	"	
Bilsborrow	Henry	25	11 Heatley	
	Mary	27	"	
	Robert	3	"	
	Alice	1	"	
Bellow	Ralph	22	2 Simpson	
Bilsborrow	Thomas	23	Talbot	
	Mary	20	"	
	Thomas	1	"	
Bains	James	57	Nr Canal W?	
Banks	Thomas	63	2 Hill	
	Ann	62	"	
	Mary	18	"	
Banks Jun	Thomas	38	4 "	
	James	9	"	
Blackburn	James		"	
Barnes	James	43	134 Friargate	
	William	21	"	
	Robert	16	"	
	James	13	"	
	Elizabeth	12	"	
	Ellen	10	"	
	Alice	7	"	
	Elizabeth	20	"	
Billington	Ann	69	134 Friargate	
Brown	Margeret	57	Backlane	

1820 Census — Catholic Congregation of Preston

Surname	Forename(s)	Age	Address	Comm
[Brown]	George	51	[Backlane]	
	Margeret	16	"	
	Richard	23	"	
Barton	Elizabeth	57	Harings Yard	
	Elizabeth	15	"	
	Robert	14	"	
Barton	Thomas	45	58 Friargate	
	Hugh	16	"	
Barton	John	36	62 "	
	Alice	39	"	
	Joseph	13	"	
	Ann	11	"	
	Matthew	9	"	
	Mary	8	"	
	Catherine	6	"	
	Ellen	5	"	
	Jane	5	"	
	Elizabeth	1	"	
Brown	John	39	76 "	
	Ann	47	"	
	Mary	14	"	
	Edward	13	"	
	Thomas	11	"	
Barnes	John	5	100 "	
Blackburn	Gregory	16	101 "	
	Vincent	14	"	
	Alice	11	"	
Bateson	Lucy	34	Claytons Yard	
Brown	Ann		7 Vauxhall	
	Alice	14	"	
	Ann	12	"	
	Margt	8	"	
	John	4	"	
	William	2	"	
Bains	James		Back Leeming St	
	Catherine	3	"	
	Mary	1	"	
	William		"	
Bains	Edward		Charlotte	
	Nancy	17	"	
	Edmund	15	"	
	Ellen	13	"	
	Peggy	10	"	
Brady	Francis		5 "	
	Elizabeth		"	
Bamber	Oswall		"	
	Ellen		"	
	Nancy		"	
Billington	Joseph		Back King St	
	Tabby		"	

1820 Census　　　　Catholic Congregation of Preston

Surname	Forename(s)	Age	Address	Comm
[Billington]	Ellen	2	[Back King St]	
	Mary	1	"	
Billington	Betty		Walton	
Bamber	Betty		"	
	Henry		"	
	Alice	19	"	
	William	17	"	
	Martha	15	"	
	John	11	"	
	Thomas	9	"	
	Betsy	7	"	
	Mary	3	"	
	Ann	13	"	
Bamber	William		Paradise	
	Ann		"	
	Ann	12	"	
	Mary	12	"	
	Margt	10	"	
	John	7	"	
	William	5	"	
	Thomas	2	"	
Brown	Ignatius		2 Back Grimshaw	
Bamber	Thomas		5 Leeming	
Billington	Mary		Back Leeming	
Bateson	John		17 King	
	Margt		"	
	Bella	4	"	
	Betty	1	"	
Booth	Hannah		French Wood	
	Ellen	11	"	
	Mary Ann	4	"	
Briley	Ellen		9 Park St	
	William	12	"	
	Richard	7	"	
Bramwell	Winifrid		Paradise	
	Sarah	3	"	
	Thomas	1	"	
Baron	Ann		"	
Banks	Thomas		24 Singletons Row	
	Betty		"	
	Isabella	16	"	
	Betty	14	"	
	Charles	12	"	
	John	11	"	
	Thomas	6	"	
	James	4	"	
	Margt	2	"	
	Mary	1	"	
Bells	Alice		6 Moor Lane	
	John	5	"	

1820 Census — Catholic Congregation of Preston

Surname	Forename(s)	Age	Address	Comm
[Bells]	Rachel	3	[Moor Lane]	
	Thomas	1	"	
Brown	John		Harrisons Hill	
	Ellen		"	
	William	15	"	
	John	13	"	
	Margt	12	"	
Bell	Hugh		Crown	
	Betty		"	
	Betty	26	"	
	Ellen	23	"	
	John	19	"	
Bolton	Nicholas		"	
	Mary		"	
	Jane	14	"	
	Ann	11	"	
	John	9	"	
	Richard	7	"	
	Mary	5	"	
	Betty	1	"	
Bell	George		"	
	Ann		"	
	John	11	"	
	Elizabeth	10	"	
	James	8	"	
	Ann	7	"	
	Mary	4	"	
	Hugh	2	"	
	Martha	1	"	
Banks	William		"	
	Ann		"	
	Joseph	19	"	
Bradley	John		Wellington	
	James		"	
Boardley	Henry		4 Singletons row	
	Grace	6	"	
	Mary	1	"	
Beasdell	Margt	20	10 Ribbleton lane	
Bleasdale	James	28	11 "	
	Wife		"	
	Mary	4	"	
	Alice	2	"	
Banks	Mary	22	12 "	
Brown	Peter	30	12 "	
Banks	James	26	23 Dale	
	William	24	"	
	Easter	1	"	
Blackburn	William	38	5 Dale Street	
	Ann	37	"	
	Alice	15	"	

85

1820 Census　　　　　　Catholic Congregation of Preston

Surname	Forename(s)	Age	Address	Comm
[Blackburn]	Richd	11	[Dale Street]	
	Elizabeth	8	"	
Banks	William	9	22　"	
	Elizabeth	32	"	
	Fanny	6	"	
Banes	Bernard	42	34　"	
	Alice	43	"	
	Thomas	21	"	
	Margeret	18	"	
	John	15	"	
	Elizabeth	14	"	
	Mary	12	"	
	William	2	"	
Billington	Thomas	19	31 Stanley	
Banks	Mary	34	6 Bengal Sq	
	Mary	12	"	
Banks	Mary	50	8　"	
	Eliza	30	"	
	James	24	"	
Brindle	John	40	6 Ferneth	
Bilington	James	46	7 Thomas	
	Catherine	43	"	
	William	19	"	
	Isabella	18	"	
	John	14	"	
	Mary	9	"	
	Catherine	7	"	
	James	4	"	
Bamber	Alice	14	11 Peter	33
	Mary	13	"	33
Bens	Richard	38	13 Frederick	
	Mary	40	"	
	John	12	"	
	Richard	8	"	
	Thomas	5	"	
	George	4	"	
	Catherine	2	"	
	Ellen	1	"	
Banks	Peter	21	42 Canal	
Batson	James	49	5 Moorside	
	Margt	50	"	
	Richard	16	"	
Batson	James	25	6　"	
	Ellen	25	"	
	John	2	"	
Batson	Mary	23	"	
	William	2	"	
Banks	Elizabeth	30	11 Canal	
	Thomas	4	"	
	William	1	"	

1820 Census　　　Catholic Congregation of Preston

Surname	Forename(s)	Age	Address	Comm
Ball	Thomas	22	16 Hope	
Billington	Thomas	30	Bk Canal	
Ball	Jane	3	16 Hope	
	Alice	1	"	
Billington	Mary	50	Bridge	
	James	25	"	
	Alice	23	"	
	John	10	"	
Banks	Thomas	74	11 "	
	Mathew	58	"	34
	John	32	"	
	Ellen	20	"	
Birchall	Alice	50	10 Birketts Place	
	Dorothy	20	"	
	Betty	17	"	
	Anthony	17	"	
Bolton	Richard	27	3 Spring	
	Elizabeth	21	"	
Bleackledg	Kitty	24	Sopery	
Bark	William	31	7 Back Lane	
	Jane	25	"	
	Margeret	1	"	
Blacow	Matthew	22	71 "	
Briers	John	17	5 Friargate	
Brown	John	44	"	
	Alice	42	"	
	James	17	"	
	Mary	11	"	
	Thomas	7	"	
	John	3	"	
Bryan	John	30	12 Hardmans Yard	
	Elizabeth	25	"	
	Thomas	6	"	
	Mary Ann	5	"	
	Sarah	1	"	
Billington	Edward	36	25 Friargate	
	Margt	29	"	
	William	4	"	
	Charles	2	"	
Banks	Joseph	29	3 Market Place	
Bell	Martha	26	"	
Barton	Lucas	14	"	
Bolton	Richard	32	Bk Horse yard	
	Mary	25	"	
	John	5	"	
	Alice	3	"	
	Ann	1	"	
Blackstock	Mary	25	28 Lune	
Brown	Nancy		Browns yard Friargate	
Bonny	Margeret	32	Friargate	

1820 Census — Catholic Congregation of Preston

Surname	Forename(s)	Age	Address	Comm
[Bonny]	Mary	5	[Friargate]	
Bradshaw	John	24	Pleasant	
Bostock	Margaret		Bostock St	
Banks	Betty		3 Pleasant	
Barton	Hugh		2 Stonygate	
	James	7	"	
	Thomas	4	"	
	John	2	"	
Banks	John		Rose	
	Mary	2	"	
Barrow	Jane	34	High	
Bragey	Mary	53	103 "	
Butler	James	26	99 "	
	Ellen	24	"	
	Mary	2	"	
Barns	Henry	32	"	
	Betty	32	"	
	Ellen	6	"	
	James	3	"	
	Thomas	2	"	
	James	53	"	
	William	18	"	
Barton	Peggy	15	12 Whitakers row	
Burk	John	50	24 Tythe Barn	
	Eliza	38	"	
	Thomas	15	"	
	Alice	13	"	
	Agnes	7	"	
	Bridget	5	"	
	John	3	"	
	Betty	1	"	
Broughem	John	60	18 Buxtons yard	
	Mary	55	"	
	Betty	20	"	
Barny	Catherine	60	13 Bishops gate	
Bamber	Margeret	43	4 Filde	
Bray	Agnes	48	"	
	Agnes	16	"	
	John	50	"	
Bilsborrow	James	49	21 Bk Kirkham	
	Alice	44	"	
	Thomas	18	"	
	Ellen	20	"	
	Richard	16	"	
	Jane	14	"	
	James	2	"	
Blackburn	Betty	75	Kirkham	
	William	21	"	
Bickerstaff	William	26	80 "	
	Eliza	24	"	

1820 Census   Catholic Congregation of Preston

Surname	Forename(s)	Age	Address	Comm
[Bickerstaff]	Ellin	3	[Kirkham]	
	Margt	1	"	
Brown	James	18	"	
	Edward	9	"	
Bilsborrow	John	23	"	
	Ann	23	"	
Barns	Richard	25	11 Gt Shaw St	
	James	13	"	
	Sarah	18	"	
Banks	Joseph	16	Vicar	
	Mary	11	"	
	William	7	"	
Barns	William	58	Vicar Street	
	Nancy	56	"	
	Richard	28	"	
	Betty	25	"	
	Alice	20	"	
	Margt	13	"	
	Ann	5	"	
Butler	Robert	35	8 Walker	
	Alice	33	"	
	Betty	10	"	
	Ann	8	"	
	John	1	"	
Barns	Margeret	11	12 "	
Baid	Mary	30	Patten Field	
	Helen	8	"	
	Thomas	5	"	
	Mary		"	
Bradley	Thomas	43	Bk Vicar St	
	Mary	42	"	
	Thomas	20	"	
	John	17	"	
	Edward	12	"	
	Richard	10	"	
	Alice	6	"	
	Agnes	3	"	
	Mary	1	"	
Blackburn	Thomas	24	Ribbleton	
	Jane	31	"	
Bolton	James	58	Marsh end	
	Catherine	58	"	
	Elizabeth	27	"	
	John	25	"	
	Catherine	22	"	
Blacow	Ellen	63		
Bradley	Robert	29	Cold Bath	
	Frances	26	"	
	James	1	"	
Bradley	John	37	Ashton Brows	

## 1820 Census	## Catholic Congregation of Preston

Surname	Forename(s)	Age	Address	Comm
[Bradley]	Ellen	27	[Ashton Brows]	
	Betty	4	"	
	Edward	2	"	
Bradley	Betty	67	Tulketh Hall	
	William	40	"	
	Betty	32	"	
	Richard	23	"	
	Betty	15	"	
Bradley	Edward	38	Water Lane end	
	Mary	43	"	
	John	9	"	
	Edward	8	"	
	Mary	6	"	
	Richard	3	"	
	William	1	"	
Billington	Richard		Fulwood	
	Ann		"	
	James		"	
	John		"	
	Betty		"	
	Robert		"	
	Edward		"	
	Margt		"	
Brewer	John		"	
	Ann		"	
	John		"	
	Robert		"	
Boys	Mary		"	
	Ann		"	
Billington	Charles		"	
Billington	Robt		11 Bread St	
Brady	James	69	Wellington	
Brady	James	29	"	
	Joseph	23	"	
	John	20	"	
Crookall	Richard	27	25 St John Street	
	Ann	28	"	
	Agnes	2	"	
	William	24	"	
	John	22	"	
Camb	John	28	Park	
	Elizabeth	35	"	
	Egnatius	6	"	
	Mary	4	"	
	Stephen	2	"	
Comprimmy	Peggy	40	5 Blue Bell yard	
Caton	Ellen	65	8 Church	
	Henry	26	"	
Crump	Margeret	16	"	
Cole	Matthew	56	55 Mince between	

1820 Census — Catholic Congregation of Preston

Surname	Forename(s)	Age	Address	Comm
[Cole]	Martha	55	[Mince between]	
	Margaret	16	"	
Carter	Ann	16	147 Church	
Crookall	Thomas	19	"	
Corbishley	John	40	5 Glovers Court	
	Ann	38	"	
	John	4	"	
	Ann	2	"	
	Elizabeth	1	"	
	Robert	14	"	
Cross	Anthony		"	
	Ann		"	
	child Mary			
Cuerdale	John	36	South Meadow lane	
	Jane	36	"	
	Elizabeth	13	"	
	Thomas	10	"	
	James	6	"	
	John	1		
Chorley	James		4 Butler St	
	Elizabeth	30	"	
	Betty	23	"	
	Richard	20	"	
	Catherine	19	"	
Crombleholme	Ann	20	7 "	
Carrol	Ann	14	71 Fishergate	
Crombleholme	Richard	24	11 St Wilfrid	
	Jane	1	"	
Chadwick	Margaret		"	
	Margaret	20	"	
Carr	Hannah	54	5 "	
	Richard	20	"	
Capstick	James	45	1 Fox	
	Prissilla	43	"	
	Thomas	18	"	
	William	17	"	
	James	14	"	
	Prissilla	13	"	
	Joseph	11	"	
	Ellen	8	"	
	Agnes	5	"	
Cornford	Ellen	15	3 Fox Street	
Cusack	Charles		Lune	
	Helen		"	
	Charles	6	"	
	Helen	4	"	
	Christopher	3	"	
	Elizabeth	1	"	
Clarkson	Elizabeth	14	111 Fishergate	
Craven	William	43	26 Mount	

1820 Census   Catholic Congregation of Preston

Surname	Forename(s)	Age	Address	Comm
[Craven]	Mary	33	[Mount]	
	John	10	"	
	Elizabeth	7	"	
Cuerdale	Henry	22	17 "	
Crombleholme	William	22	11 "	
	David	14	"	
Cornthwaite	Jane	25	end of Chapel St	
Cuerden	Mathew		1 Mount Pleasant	
	Betty	17	"	
	Mathew	16	"	
	Sally	14	"	
	Mary	9	"	
	William	7	"	
Campell	John	20	15 Heatley	
Cowell	Robert	25	18 "	
Clarkson	Isabella	46	"	
Caton	William	31	7 Simpson	
	Henry	5	"	
	Cuthbert	3	"	
	Thomas	1	"	
Cottam	Ellis	23	3 "	
	Elizabeth	21	"	
	John	3	"	
	Alice	1	"	
	Esabella	21	9 "	
	Jane	26	"	
	Margeret	11	"	
	Mary	6	"	
Coup	Ann	21	7 "	
	William	2	"	
Coup	John	43	6 Ratcliff	
	John	9	"	
	Thomas	7	"	
	William	3	"	
	Margeret	1	"	
Cerrill	William	29	16 "	
Carter	James	50	36 Friargate	
	Ann	24	"	
	Dorothy	20	"	
	Robert	18	"	
	Richard	16	"	
	William	10	"	
Cormick	Andrew	33	13 Hill St	
Clark	Mary	45	Friargate	
Cross	Joseph	22	135 "	
	Jane	20	"	
Cardwell	Richard		-	
Challinor	Thomas	46	Union	
	Alice	49	"	
	William	17	"	

1820 Census — Catholic Congregation of Preston

Surname	Forename(s)	Age	Address	Comm
Cambell	Rebecca	25	[Union]	
	John	13	"	
	Elizabeth	11	"	
	George	7	"	
	Maria	5	"	
Counsel	Dorothy	60	58 Friargate	
Carter	Thomas	45	61 "	
	Alice	42	"	35
	John	17	"	
Counsel	Margt	39	65 "	
Cowper	Ann	75	127 "	
Crombleholme	John	19	128 "	
Champion	Thomas	6	3 Vauxhall road	
Clemming	Richard		9 "	
	Alice		"	
	Ann	6	"	
	Elizabeth	1	"	
Catterall	John		Oak	
	Mary		"	
	James	10	"	
	John	8	"	
	Ellen	7	"	
	Mary	4	"	
	Betty	1	"	
Crook	Richard		Charlotte	
	Margt		"	
	John	7	"	
	William	4	"	
	Bridget	1	"	
Cunningham	Hy		Bk King	
Calvert	Edward		William	
Cottam	Thomas		"	
	Jane		"	
	Cuthbert	13	"	
Carter	Betty		Paradise	
Cliff	Ann		1 Queen Street	
	Thomas	12	"	
	James	8	"	
Cook	Joseph		26 Willow	
	Alice		"	
	Nancy	5	"	
Cammell	Nancy		7 Back Willow	
	Mary	20	"	
	Edward	15	"	
	Ann	11	"	
	Margt	9	"	
	John	8	"	
	Grace	5	"	
Coup	James		1 Princess	
	Mary		"	

1820 Census Catholic Congregation of Preston

Surname	Forename(s)	Age	Address	Comm
[Coup]	Sarah	13	[Princess]	
	Thomas	12	"	
	Margt	6	"	
	Ellen	3	"	
	John	1	"	
Coup	John		12 King	
	Mary		"	
	Ellen		"	
	John		"	
Coup	John		Paradise	
	Alice		"	
Coup	Robert		Singletons Row	
	Jane		"	
	George	5	"	
	Ellen	2	"	
	John	1	"	
Connal	Thomas		Craggs Court	
	Ch		"	
	Betty	10	"	
	Margeret	5	"	
Comyleach	George		"	
	Ellen		"	
	Henry	19	"	
	George	14	"	
	John	8	"	
	Ellen	7	"	
	Daniel	4	"	
Catteral	John		Moore lane	
	Ann		"	
	Thomas	17	"	
	John	6	"	
	Ann	4	"	
	Alice	2	"	
Crook	Thomas		Crows St	
	Sarah		"	
	James	3	"	
	William	5	"	
Cockerin	Ann		"	36
Caton	William	35	"	
	Mary		"	
	Ellen	9	"	
	Jane	8	"	
	Richard	5	"	
	Catherine	1	"	
Crook	Thomas	32	1 Ribbleton Lane	
	Mary	37	"	
	Margeret	11	"	
	John	9	"	
	George	7	"	
	William	5	"	

1820 Census — Catholic Congregation of Preston

Surname	Forename(s)	Age	Address	Comm
[Crook]	Thomas	2	[Ribbleton Lane]	
Crook	Thomas	34	2 "	
	Ellen	33	"	
	William	10	"	
	Guels	8	"	
	Bibby	6	"	
	Mary Ann	5	"	
	Edward	3	"	
	John	2	"	
Catteral	James	32	12 "	
	Mary	26	"	
	Lucy	2	"	
Cowell	John	34	3 Bengal Sq	
	Nancy	30	"	
	William	6	"	
	Margt	3	"	
	George	1	"	
Cliff	Ellen	22	6 "	
Collison	Sarah	25	16 Holdens Square	
Carrol	William	60	9 Thomas	
	Jonas	18	"	
	Mary	17	"	
Clarkson	Ellen	60	9 Elizabeth	
	John	36	"	
	Ellen	30	"	
	Mary	8	"	
	William	1	"	
Coape	Joseph	32	4 Moorside	
	Ann	30	"	
	Mary	9	"	
	John	6	"	
	Joseph	4	"	
	Ann	2	"	
	Agnes	1	"	
Close	Mathew	34	44 Canal	
	Mary	14	"	
	Jane	12	"	
	John	10	"	
	Betty	8	"	
	Matthew	1	"	
Catmeal	Thomas	37	5 "	
	Alice	41	"	
	John	2	"	
Cross	William	29	25 "	
	Alice	26	"	
	William	5	"	
	Richard	3	"	
	Mary	1	"	
Cooper	Jane	43	21 "	
	John	17	"	

1820 Census　　　　Catholic Congregation of Preston

Surname	Forename(s)	Age	Address	Comm
[Cooper]	Thomas	16	[Canal]	
	Betty	14	"	
	Henry	11	"	
	Richard	9	"	
	Mary	5	"	
	Peter	3	"	
Cellat	Thomas	50	Fosters Square	
	John	18	"	
	Thomas	16	"	
Cormal	William	49	Bk Canal	
	Mary	49	"	
	Jane	11	"	
Cuerdale	Mathew	26	37 Bridge	
	Sarah	82	"	
	Sarah	15	"	
	Mathew	15	"	
	Richard	12	"	
Cottam	John	62	5 Berketts Place	
	Jane	58	"	
	Ann	14	"	
	John	12	"	
	George	11	"	
Catteral	William	35	15 Bridge Street Lane	
	Sarah	65	"	
	William	3	"	
	Mary	1	"	
Cornthwaite	William	31	11 "	
	Elizabeth	26	"	
	Robert	2	"	
	William	1	"	
Crann	John	45	21 "	
	Mary	41	"	
	Ann	19	"	
	Edward	17	"	
	John	14	"	
	Mary	12	"	
	Elizabeth	9	"	
Crann	Giles	75	"	
Cuerdale	Henry	83	"	
	Betty	75	"	
	Thomas	32	"	
	Mary	29	"	
	Margt	7	"	
	Henry	5	"	
	William	3	"	
	Elizabeth	1	"	
Clayton	Alexander	51	1 Sopery	
	Margeret	48	"	
	Margeret	22	"	
	Thomas	19	"	

1820 Census Catholic Congregation of Preston

Surname	Forename(s)	Age	Address	Comm
[Clayton]	Richard	17	[Sopery]	
	John	15	"	
	William	13	"	
	Alexander	8	"	
	Laurence	6	"	
Cellet	Thomas	42	Fosters Square	
	John	18	"	
	Thomas	16	"	
Crook	John	8	9 Back Lane	
Cooper	-		Back Horse Yard	
Chorley	James	27	Friargate	
	Ellen	30	"	
	James	1	"	
Cook	Peggy		Sike Hill	
Clayton	William	45	3 Shambles	
	Elizabeth	44	"	
	Dorothy	18	"	
	Elizabeth	17	"	
	James	14	"	
	William	12	"	
	Jane	7	"	
	Sarah	5	"	
	Hannah	4	"	
Clayton	James	36	11 "	
	Margt	31	"	
	John	10	"	
	Dorothy	9	"	
	Richard	8	"	
	Margt	6	"	
	James	1	"	
Clayton	Richard	76	11 "	
Chew	John	47	"	
	Mary	63	"	
	John	24	"	
	Joseph	20	"	
Clarkson	Thomas	25	"	
	Nancy	31	"	
	Mary	5	"	
	Margt	3	"	
	Thomas	1	"	
Caddy	Nancy	14	Molyneux Square	
Catteral	Sarah		Waterworths yard	
Cooper	Elizabeth	58	3 Slaters yard	
Corling	Betsy	20	Friargate (at Bull Inn)	
Cookson	Ann	16	170 Friargate	
Connel	John	52	Holdens Square	
	Ann	50	"	
	Bridget	21	"	
	Eliza	10	"	
	Catherine	13	"	

1820 Census Catholic Congregation of Preston

Surname	Forename(s)	Age	Address	Comm
[Connel]	Thomas	1	[Holdens Square]	
Catteral	Isabella		56 Pleasant	
Crombleholme	Mrs	45	"	
	James		"	
	Ellen		"	
Calvert	Mrs	27	"	
	John	2	"	
Curry	John	23	"	
	Jane		"	
	Charles	15	"	
Craven	Richard		51 Pleasant	
	Sarah		"	
	Henry		"	
	John	14	"	
Crombleholme	David		Library	
	Alice		"	
	Thomas	10	"	
	Ellen	4	"	
	Mary	1	"	
Cockrel	Mary		Rose	
Clarkson	George		"	
	Margt		"	
	Miss	20	"	
	Elizabeth	17	"	
	Nicholas	15	"	
	Mr	22	"	
	Mary	13	"	
	Ann	10	"	
	Margeret	7	"	
Carrol	John	6	50 High	
Crane	Mary	17	"	
Cromby	Lucy	15	"	
Canry	William	60	19 "	
Canry	Ellen	49	"	
	William	18	"	
	Bridget	9	"	
	Mary	7	"	
	Nathaniel	5	"	
Croce	Edward	20	103 "	
Caddy	Jonathan	39	21 "	
	Mary	38	"	
	John	15	"	
	Betty	12	"	
	Mary	9	"	
	Nancy	13	"	
Clarkson	Betty	53	Whittakers row	
	Thomas	20	"	
	Robert	14	"	
Clarkson	Betty	51	12 "	
Cane	James	34	6 Tythe Barn	

1820 Census — Catholic Congregation of Preston

Surname	Forename(s)	Age	Address	Comm
[Cane]	Eliza	26	[Tythe Barn]	
	John	5	"	
	Thomas	1	"	
Clayton	Edward	80	Buxtons yard	
Cook	Eliza	82	7 Filde	
Crombleholme	Matt	45	24 Bk Kirkham	
	Mary	42	"	
	John	18	"	
	Thomas	16	"	
	Winifrid	13	"	
	Richard	10	"	
Cummabach	Henry	20	"	
Connell	Thomas	20	6 "	
	Ellen	22	"	
Cronshall	Peter	50	6 Kirkham	
	Betty	25	"	
	Ann	10	"	
	Betty	8	"	
	Mary	5	"	
	Ann	17	"	
Corcoran	Patrick	54	9 Snowhill	
	Frances	54	"	
	Nic	15	"	
Corwan	Ann	23	13 Vicar	
	Ellen	4	"	
	Gennie	2	"	
	Ann	1	"	
Caton	Robert	39	"	
	Elizabeth	35	"	
	James	15	"	
	William	13	"	
	Betty	11	"	
	Bella	9	"	
	John	7	"	
	Thomas	5	"	
	Robert	3	"	
Cross	John	29	"	
	Ann	23	"	
	Alexander		"	
Charnock	Betty	52	4 Walker	
Caton	William	68	12 "	
	Jane	62	"	
	Robert	26	"	
	Bella	24	"	
Cook	Helen	24	"	
	Edward	2	"	
	James	1	"	
Carlin	John	51	30 Walker Street	
	Alice	41	"	
	Margt	22	"	

1820 Census　　　　　　**Catholic Congregation of Preston**

Surname	Forename(s)	Age	Address	Comm
[Carlin]	Richard	15	[Walker Street]	
	Nancy	2	"	
	John	6	"	
	William	4	"	
	Joseph	2	"	
	Lucy	1	"	
Chew	Richard	31	Ribbleton	
	Ann	25	"	
	Elizabeth	63	"	
Cook	John	38	"	
	Betty	38	"	
	Betty	10	"	
	Margt	7	"	
	Helen	5	"	
	Mary	3	"	
Cook	Mary	77	"	
	Henry	24	"	
Carlisle	John	45	Marsh end	
	Mary	35	"	
Cottam	Lucy	21	Nr Tulketh hall at Stocks	
Clarkson	Thomas	32	Marsh end	
	Ellen	28	"	
	Alice	4	"	
	Ann	1	"	
Coupe	Thomas	27	Greaves town	
Cuerden	Matthew	50	"	
	Mary	50	"	
	John	24	"	
	Betty	18	"	
	Ellen	16	"	
	James	12	"	
	Mary	10	"	
	Peggy	7	"	
	Thomas	8	"	
Crook	Edward	30	Long Lane	
	Mary	26	"	
Clarkson	Edward		Fulwood	
	Jane		"	
	John		"	
	James		"	
	Robert		"	
	Ann		"	
	Thomas		"	
	Betty		"	
Clarkson	Thomas		"	
	Ann		"	
	Ellen		"	
	John		"	
	Robert		"	
	Bella		"	

1820 Census — Catholic Congregation of Preston

Surname	Forename(s)	Age	Address	Comm
[Clarkson]	Mary		[Fulwood]	
	Thomas		"	
	Sally		"	
Chew	Thomas		"	
	John		"	
	Ann		"	
	Ann		"	
Cannock	Joseph		"	
	Ann		"	
	Mary		"	
	Betty		"	
	Peter		"	
	Edward		"	
	William		"	
	Thomas		"	
	Joseph			
Crook	Thomas		2 Mountpleasant	
	Margret		"	
	Winifrid		"	
	John		"	
	Ann		"	
	Jane		"	
	Ellen		"	
	Ralph		"	
	Thomas		"	
	Henry	3	"	
	Margt	1	"	
	James			
Dilworth	Joseph	46	9 St John St	
	Jane	46	"	
	Mary	22	"	
	John	20	"	
	Henry	18	"	
	William	16	"	
	Margeret	12	"	
	Joseph	7	"	
	James	4	"	
	Alice	1	"	
Dent	William	27	17 Nile	
	Mary	27	"	
	William	7	"	
	Ann	4	"	
Dilworth	William	23	17 Cotton Court	
	Ann	25	"	
	Mary	5	"	
	Alice	4	"	
	Jane	1	"	
Duckworth	Richard	40	20 Mince between	
	Hannah	39	"	
	Elizabeth	14	"	

1820 Census   Catholic Congregation of Preston

Surname	Forename(s)	Age	Address	Comm
[Duckworth]	Mary	12	[Mince between]	
	Richard	8	"	
	Alice	5	"	
	Thomas	1	"	
Dobson	William	55	115 Church	
	Elizabeth	32	"	
	Robert	8	"	
	Mary	7	"	
	Mason	5	"	
	Jane	3	"	
	Francis	2	"	
Dilworth	James	17	6 Woodcocks yard	
Dobson	Elizabeth	33	58 Fishergate	
Dobson	Thomas	5	11 Mount	
Darlington	Sicily	21	3 Well	
Dickinson	John	50	20 Heatley	
	Ellen	55	"	
	Ann	27	"	
	Mary	26	"	
	Margeret	21	"	
	Betty	17	"	
	William	15	"	
	Alice	12	"	
	Joseph	10	"	
Dewhurst	Peter	41	Simpson	
	Ann	46	"	
	John	14	"	
	Richard	12	"	
	Mary Ann	9	"	
Draper	Mary	36	3 Hill St	
	Ellen	16	"	
	Elizabeth	14	"	
	James	12	"	
	William	10	"	
	Thomas	7	"	
	Richard	4	"	
	Mary	2	"	
Duckett	Richard	38	37 Friargate	
	Mary	38	"	
	James	11	"	
	Jane	9	"	
	Ann	7	"	
	Richard	5	"	
	Mary	3	"	
	Elizabeth	1	"	
Dickinson	James	46	50 "	
	Martha	51	"	
	Peter	18	"	
	William	15	"	
	Thomas	12	"	

1820 Census   Catholic Congregation of Preston

Surname	Forename(s)	Age	Address	Comm
[Dickinson]	Ann	10	[Friargate]	
Dunn	Joseph	52	"	
	Bridget	19	"	
	John	12	"	
	Elizabeth	8	"	
	James	4	"	
Daniel	Elizabeth	46	137 "	
	Joseph	16	"	
	John	14	"	
Dewhurst	Catherine	62	97 "	
Dodds	Joseph	61	123 "	
	Elizabeth	39	"	
	Mary	30	"	
	Elizabeth	28	"	
Dunderdale	Mary		9 Charlotte	
	Thomas		"	
	Richard		"	
	William	18	"	
	James	16	"	
	Alice		"	
	John	15	"	
	Joseph	12	"	
	Ann	9	"	
	Vincent	6	"	
Duffy	James		King	
	Margaret		"	
	Francis	5	"	
	James	1	"	
Dawson	Alice		Back King	
Donnighty	Richard		12 King	
Duffin	James		28 "	
	Frank	5	"	
	James	2	"	
Dewhurst	Ann		38 Singleton row	
Dawson	James		"	
	Ann		"	
	Thomas	1	"	
Davis	Mary		3 Moore lane	
	Anthony	1	"	
Dickinson	Thomas		9 Crown	
	Jane		"	
	Ann	8	"	
	William	6	"	
	Joseph	4	"	
Devling	John		"	
	Ann		"	
	Mary	11	"	
	James	6	"	
	Ellen	4	"	
Dugan	William		"	

1820 Census　　　　Catholic Congregation of Preston

Surname	Forename(s)	Age	Address	Comm
Develing	Bridget		Crows	
	Ellen	14	"	
	Ann	10	"	
	Bridget	4	"	
	Daniel	1	"	
Develing	Daniel	24	8 Ribbleton Lane	
Darwin	William	64	9 Elizabeth	
	Mary	30	"	
	Ann	8	"	
	Mary	4	"	
Darwin	John	28	"	
	Mary	26	"	
	William	3	"	
	Richard	1	"	
Davis	Thomas	62	Canal	
	Mary	47	"	
Donley	Charles	38	Bk Canal	
	Sarah	35	"	
	John	14	"	
	Ann	6	"	
	Francis	2	"	
	Mary	2	"	
Dunn	Elizabeth	63	Hope	
Dunn	Patrick	70	Hope Street	
Dewhurst	Adam	34	7 Bridge	
	Catherine	35	"	
	Richard	6	"	
	Thomas	4	"	
	George	6	"	
	James	6	"	
Davis	Sally	22	14 Spring St	
Dunderdale	Richard	24	Fosters Square	
	Margt	30	"	
	Thomas	2	"	
	James	1	"	
Duckett	George		Friday St	
	Mary		"	
	James	7	"	
	Ann	1	"	
Dunderdale	Robert		"	
	Jane		"	
	Robert	15	"	
	Alice	9	"	
Dayley	John	40	25 Market Place	
Dawson	James		46 Pleasant	
	Jane		"	
	J.C.	2	"	
	Sicely	1	"	
Digles	Charles		Bottom of Cock Yard	
	Margeret		"	

1820 Census — Catholic Congregation of Preston

Surname	Forename(s)	Age	Address	Comm
[Digles]	William	9	[Bottom of Cock Yard]	
	George	7	"	
	Hugh	5	"	
	Mary	11	"	
Dunn	Christopher	50	101 High	
	Catherine	45	"	
	Ann	15	"	
	Michal	7	"	
	Easter	1	"	
Dolphin	John	29	22 "	
	Ellen	30	"	
	Richard		"	
	Fanny		"	
Dixon	Mary	27	27 Tythe Barn St	
	Thomas	2	"	
Dobson	Lawrence	57	7 Tythe Barn	37
	Peggy	46	"	
	James	26	"	
	Joseph	21	"	
	John	19	"	
	Mary	11	"	
	Henry	9	"	
	Lawrence	6		
Dickinson	John	40	13 Bishopsgate	37
	Peggy	13	"	
	Betty	11	"	
	Mary	9	"	
	Christopher	7	"	
	Ann	5	"	
	Henry	2	"	
Dagger	Ann	40	7 Filde	
	Ellen	20	"	
	Friday	14	"	
	Eliza	5	"	
Dewhurst	John	36	"	
	Alice	33	"	
	Richard	14	"	
	Ann	13	"	
	James	11	"	
	John	8	"	
	William	6	"	
	Robert	1	"	
Dunderdale	Richd	28	2 Bolton	
	Betty	19	"	
	Mary	22	"	
Derome	Mary	38	6 Snow Hill	
	Elizabeth	9	"	
	Joseph	6	"	
	Thomas	5	"	
	John	3	"	

1820 Census   Catholic Congregation of Preston

Surname	Forename(s)	Age	Address	Comm
Delapes	John	38	34 [Snow Hill]	
	Mary	50	"	
	Ellen	11	"	
	Amelia	9	"	
	Margt	7	"	
	Stephen	5	"	
	Catherine	1	"	
Dickinson	Thomas	39	36 Snow hill	
	John	11	"	
	William	9	"	
	Bella	6	"	
	Thomas	1	"	
Dawson	Thomas	53	5 Vicars	
	Alice	53	"	
	Alice	17	"	
Duckworth	Margt	36	"	
	Bella	6	"	
Dunderdale	Thomas	29	7 "	
	Helen	19	"	
	Ann	2	"	
	William	1	"	
Dunderdale	Ann	61	11 Walker	
	Bella	40	"	
	Mary	21	"	
Dagger	Agnes	20	Ashton Brows	
Dawson	William	21	"	
Dewhurst	John		Fulwood	
	James		"	
	Ann		"	
	Ann		"	
	Richard		"	
	Betty		"	
	Robert		"	
Dickinson	William		"	
Edmondson	Richard	24	7 Nile Street	
	Ann	25	"	
	Mary	15	23 Church	
Eccles	Margaret	22	"	
Emus	John	18	6 Woodcocks yard	
	Mary	22	"	
Easterby	Isabella	36	4 Theatre	
	Richard	16	"	
Eccles	Ellen	24	71 Fishergate	
	Sarah	53	16 Chapel	
Ellis	Thomas	40	10 Mount Pleasant	
	Margeret	45	"	
	Ellen	17	"	
	Robert	16	"	
	John	15		
	Eliza	13	"	

1820 Census — Catholic Congregation of Preston

Surname	Forename(s)	Age	Address	Comm
[Ellis]	Thomas	10	[Mount Pleasant]	
	Mary	6	"	
Eccles	Ann	48	Simpson	
	Ann	8	"	
	George	7	"	
Elm	John		Oak	
	Ellen		"	
	Mary	4	"	
	Edmund	2	"	
	Ann	1	"	
Erwin	Hannah		Bk King	
	John		"	
	Betty		"	
Eastham	Thomas		Crows St	
	Margeret		"	
	Thomas	15	"	
	Edward	10	"	
	Mary	9	"	
	Robert	4	"	
	William	3	"	
Eccles	Ellin		"	
	Alice		"	
Erstum	Thomas	50	3 Frederick	
	Jane	55	"	
	Joseph	16	"	
	Mary	14	"	
	Nancy	10	"	
	Maria	6	"	
Eays	Christopher	60	42 Canal	
	Mary	18	"	
Eccles	Betty	45	3 Bridge	
	Joseph	17	"	
	John	8	"	
Eves	William	30	27 Friargate	
Eccles	James	35	"	
	Betsy	40	"	
	James	12	"	
	Ellin	10	"	
	Mary	7	"	
	Thomas	5	"	
	James	1	"	
Eastwood	Mary	50	28 Lune	
Even	Ellen	6	2 Stonygate	
Eastwood	Eliza		Avenham	
	Ann		"	
	Ruth	12	"	
	William		"	
Edmondson	Elizabeth	49	32 Whitakers row	
Eccleston	Ann	26	"	
	Margt	24	"	

1820 Census   Catholic Congregation of Preston

Surname	Forename(s)	Age	Address	Comm
[Eccleston]	William	23	[Whitakers row]	
Eastwood	Ellen	40	5 Buxtons yard	
	Ellen	13	"	
	Dorothy	9	"	
	Jane	9	"	
	William	3	"	
Eccles	James	24	16 Filde	
	Jane	24	"	
	Ann	3	"	
	John	1	"	
Eccles	Matthew	50	16 Bolton St	
	Ann	55	"	
	Lawrence	18	"	
	Ann	15	"	
	William	11	"	
	George	9	"	
Eccles	John	27	"	
	Betty	28	"	
	Ann	5	"	
	Ellen	4	"	
	Jane	2	"	
	Charles	1	"	
Edwards	John	28	21 Snow hill	
	Nancy	25	"	
	Betty	1	"	
Eccleston	Ellin	17	Vicar St	
Eccles	Thomas	49	31 "	
	Nancy	49	"	
	Jane	13	"	
	John	11	"	
	Richard	10	"	
	George	5	"	
Eastham	Robert	24	19 Walker	
	Alice	23	"	
	Bella	30	"	
	John		"	
	Thomas	1	"	
Eaves	John		Fulwood	
	Thomison		"	
	James		"	
	Matthew		"	
	Ann		"	
	Mary		"	
Eaves	John		"	
	Bridget		"	
	Ann		"	
Felton	Margeret	19	25 St John St	
Forrest	Margeret	20	28 Church	
Farrer	Mary	23	3 Church	38
	Jane	1	"	

1820 Census Catholic Congregation of Preston

Surname	Forename(s)	Age	Address	Comm
Fearnside	Nancy	46	33 Mince between	
Franks	Peggy	59	6 Woodcocks yard	
Fox	Alice	38	42 Fishergate	
Fisher	Martha	62	"	
Friar	John		1 West End	
	Margeret M		"	
	Margeret		"	
Farrington	Ellen	27	6 Mount Pleasant	
	William	7	"	
	Catherine	5	"	
Fox	Richard	24	22 Heatley	
Finch	Thomas	41	1 Simpson	
Fairclough	Robert	38	4 Hill	
	Alice	34	"	
	John	7	"	
	Cuthbert	5	"	
	Ann	2	"	
Farnworth	Henry	59	3 "	
	Dorothy	54	"	
	John	31	"	
Fox	John	50	Back Lane	
	Mary	35	"	
	Margt	12	"	
	John	10	"	
	Mary Ann	8	"	
	Charles	4	"	
Fhent	Richard		Bk Charlotte	39
	Nancy		"	
	William	21	"	
	Richard	11	"	
	Mary	8	"	
	Ann	4	"	
Forrest	Betty		23 Willow	
Frank	James	5	28 King	
Fairclough	Richd		Paradise	
	Thomas		"	
	Margt			
Fishwick	Betty		Moore lane	
Finch	Mr		"	
	Betty		"	
	Sarah	10	"	
	Mary	9	"	
	John	1	"	
Fryer	Phaelix		"	
	Mary		"	
	Margt	12	"	
	Mary	5	"	
	John	4	"	
	Peter	2	"	
Fishwick	Betty		Crows St	

1820 Census   Catholic Congregation of Preston

Surname	Forename(s)	Age	Address	Comm
[Fishwick]	Sarah	10	[Crows St]	
	Mary	9	"	
	John	1	"	
Furnifer	William		17 North St	
	Ellen		"	
	Mary	21	"	
	Betty	18	"	
	Margt	16	"	
	Ellen	10	"	
	Easter	9	"	
	Agnes	6	"	
	John	4	"	
	Ann	1	"	
Fiswick	John	25	13 Bk Canal	
	Calvan	26	"	
	William	6	"	
	Mary	4	"	
	Robert	1	"	
Flood	Michal	37	3 Hope	
	Thomas	15	"	
	Mary	4	"	
	Ann	10	"	
Faire	Jane	25	6 Friargate	
Frankland	Joss	35	18 Shambles	
	Ann	32	"	
	James	8	"	
	Thomas	7	"	
	Ann	5	"	
	Ellen	3	"	
	Jane	1	"	
Fishwick	Emma	16	9 M'ket Place	
Fisher	Betty	40	167 Friargate	
Forrest	James	26	Library St	
Fairclough	Jane	32	26 Bk Kirkham	
Frazer	Jane	44	10 "	
	Catherine	15	"	
	Eliza	17	"	
Flanigan	Betty	75	12 Kirkham	
Fazakerly	Ellen	41	4 Kirkham St	
	John	18	"	
	Charles	7	"	
	Joseph	2	"	
Fazakerly	James	64	6 Walker	
	Ann	58	"	
Fair	John	36	Five lane ends	
	Mary	39	"	
	James	7	"	
	Mary	4	"	
	John	2	"	
Furnilove	John		Fulwood	

1820 Census Catholic Congregation of Preston

Surname	Forename(s)	Age	Address	Comm
[Furnilove]	Betty		[Fulwood]	
	James		"	
	Robert		"	
	Ann		"	
	John		"	
	William		"	
Farmer	John		"	
Forrest	John		"	
	Ann		"	
	George		"	
	James		"	
	John		"	
	Richard		"	
	William		"	
	Ellen		"	
	Martha		"	
	Margt		"	
	Bella		"	
	Thomas		"	
	Alice		"	
Garstang	John	80	10 Holdens Yard	
Garth	Margeret	42	10 Cockyard	
Goodier	Margeret	65	Evenham	
Gillow	Thomas	15	147 Church	
Grave	Elizabeth	20	40 Fishergate	
Gradwell	George		41 "	
	Mary		"	
	Mary Ann	3w	"	
Green	Mary	28	5 Willow Place	
Gradwell	Alice	66	4 "	
Gillibrand	Eliza		58 Fishergate	
Gillow	Joseph	40	1 St Wilfrid	
	Ann	40	"	
	Alice	15	"	
	Isabella	12	"	
	Ellen	9	"	
	Elizabeth	7	"	
	Margeret	3	"	
Gradwell	Richard	45	6 Lune	
	Jane	44	"	
	Margeret	20	"	
	Esther	16	"	
Gravewell	Mary	62	39 Mount	
	Jane	33		
Gillett	Richard	55	35 "	
Geread	Ann	77	16 Chapel	
Garrett	Henry	27	7 Chandler	
	Mary	25	"	
Grimshaw	Ellen	45	13 Heatley	
Gillow	William	21	14 Ratcliffe	

111

1820 Census   Catholic Congregation of Preston

Surname	Forename(s)	Age	Address	Comm
Gradwell	John	33	36 Friargate	
	Isabella	21	"	
	Richard	9	"	
	John	7	"	
	Joseph	1	"	
Gardiner	Lucy	12	"	
Geldart	Ann	19	3 Hill	
Gradwell	Joseph	35	5 "	
	Eliza	34	"	
	Cicily	11	"	
	John	10	"	
Gillow Snr	Robt	37	37 "	
	Mary	35		
	Robert	12	"	
	Elizabeth	10	"	
	William	8	"	
	Winifrid	6	"	
	Mary Ann	4	"	
Grayson	Margeret	16	37 "	
Gradwell	Ann	9	5 "	
	Lawrence	6	"	
	Jane	4	"	
	William	2	"	
Gradwell	James	40	50 Friargate	
	William	2	"	
	Jane	1	"	
Gorton	Thomas	22	"	
Gregson	Henry	57	135 "	
	Mary	52	"	
	Richard	18	"	
	Thomas	15	"	
	John	11	"	
	Mary	9	"	
Green	William	24	Back Lane	
	Agnes	22	"	
	Ann	1	"	
Goff	Joseph	34	"	
	John	12	"	
	Thomas	7	"	
	Bridgett	5	"	
	Agnes	2	"	
	Joseph	1	"	
Gregson	Jane	66	51 Friargate	
	Henry	52	"	
Goodier	Joseph	51	70 "	
	Esther	47	"	
	Thomas	17	"	
	Robert	7	"	
Grime	John	16	100 "	
Goodier	John	23	4 Prescotts yard	

1820 Census — Catholic Congregation of Preston

Surname	Forename(s)	Age	Address	Comm
[Goodier]	Ann	23	[Prescotts yard]	
	Ann	3	"	
	Joseph	2	"	
	Henry	1	"	
Gilmore	Elizabeth	50	127 "	
Gillow	George	18	128 Friargate	
Gray	John		26 Vauxhall	
	Thomas		"	
	Elizabeth	20	"	
	John	17	"	
	George	11	"	
	Orselagh	8	"	
	William	5	"	
	James	3	"	
Gordon	A		Oak	
	Catherine		"	
	Mary	20	"	
	Peter	17	"	
	Catherine	16	"	
	George	11	"	
	Nancy	9	"	
	Barnaby	6	"	
Glover	Joseph		6 Charlotte	
	Ellen		"	
	Edward		"	
Gregson	John		28 Charlotte	
Gardner	John		Walton	
	Mary		"	
	Nicholas		"	
	John		"	
	Mary		"	
	Margt		"	
Grimminson	Mrs			
Gardner	Henry		Paradise	
	Jane		"	
	John		"	
Gardner	Edward		"	40
	Joseph		"	
	Thomas		"	
	Mary		"	
Greatson	Mary		Paradise	
Gregson	Edward		Singletons Row	
	John	21		
Gripping	Francis		Moore lane	
	Jane		"	
Gardner	John		Harrison Hill	
	Jane		"	
	Ann	17	"	
	Jane	13	"	
	Mary	10	"	

1820 Census — Catholic Congregation of Preston

Surname	Forename(s)	Age	Address	Comm
[Gardner]	Betty	8	[Harrison Hill]	
	John	5	"	
Gaskel	Ann		"	
	Ellen	2	"	
	Betty	1	"	
Gaskel	Elizabeth	48	11 Canal	
Green	John	21	Hope	
	Hannah	21	"	
Gold	James	79	24 Bridge	
	Mary	60	"	
	Mary	30	"	
	Betty	29	"	
	Jane	22	"	
	Margt	24	"	
Gillat	William	60	Birketts Place	
	Mary	55	"	
	Margt	19	"	
	Richard	15	"	
	Matthew	13	"	
	Nancy	11	"	
	Betty	9	"	
	Ellen	4	"	
	Catherine	2	"	
Gradwell	John	64	16 Bridge St Lane	
	Jane	67	"	
Gradwell	William	30	16 "	
	Margt	30	"	
Gregson	Robert	85	"	
	John	44	"	
Greenough	Mr	22	5 Friargate	
Gornal	Agnes	42	28 Shambles	
Gregson	Edward	32	Gin Bow entry	
Gordon	Ellen		41 Pleasant	
Gordon	James	5	Rose	41
Greenham	Robert		Avenham	
	Hannah		"	
Ganen	Bryan	61	36 High	
	Winifrid	52	"	
	Adam	43	"	
	Winifrid	2	"	
Glover	Mr		Everton Gardens	
	Mrs		"	
	Ellen	11	"	
	Ann	6	"	
	Alice	1	"	
Grundy	Alice	54	9 Filde	
	Charles	17	"	
	Edward	15	"	
	Richard	14	"	
	Alice	20	"	

1820 Census   Catholic Congregation of Preston

Surname	Forename(s)	Age	Address	Comm
[Grundy]	Henry	9	[Filde]	
	Mary	7	"	
	Ellen	1	"	
Grayson	Ann	51	10 "	
Gillat	Nicholas	35	1 Bolton St	
	Mary	26	"	
Gardner	Thomas	29	2 Vicar St	
	Margt	28	"	
	Mary	5	"	
	Jane	3	"	
	Robert	1	"	
Green	William	58	6 Patten Street	
	Alice	46	"	
	Thomas	19	"	
	Alice	12	"	
	Mary	10	"	
	Charles	5	"	
	Catherine		"	
Gordon	Peter		Fulwood	
	Margt		"	
Greaves	Thomas	28	2 Mounce St	
	Ann	29	"	
	Elizabeth		"	
Hayes	James	44	10 St John Street	
	Sarah	36	"	
	William	15	"	
	Nicholas	13	"	
	Mary Ann	11	"	
	John	9	"	
	James	6	"	
	Peter	3	"	
	Charles	1	"	
Horrock	Samuel	70	11 "	
	Fanny	66	"	
	William	24	"	
	John	16	"	
	Sicily	31	"	
	Fanny	22	"	
	Margeret	19	"	
Hatherton	Sarah	35	7 Blue Bell yard	
Heaton	Lawrence	48	12 Holden Yard	
	Betty	34	"	
Holyday	William	47	98 Church	
	Ann	41	"	
	Thomas	17	"	
	Charles	14	"	
	Jane	12	"	
	Mary Ann	9	"	
	Ann	6	"	
	Elizabeth	4	"	

1820 Census   Catholic Congregation of Preston

Surname	Forename(s)	Age	Address	Comm
Holmes	William	32	23 [Church]	
	Ellen	31	"	
	Ann	6	"	
	Mary	5	"	
	Robert	3	"	
	Ellen	1	"	
Harrison	Betty	70	4 Mince between	
Higginson	Robert	35	"	
	Betty	34	"	
	Thomas	6	"	
	Alice	2	"	
	Mary	1	"	
Hood	Jane	22	42 Fishergate	
Hall	Mary	60	5 Theatre	
	Ann	22	"	
	Elizabeth	16	"	
Horn	Mary	19	41 Fishergate	
Hodgson	Isabella	28	69 "	
Higginson	Thomas	36	85 "	
	James	3	"	
	Frederick	1	"	
Harrison	Mary		11 St Wilfrid	
Horn	John	30	"	
Haggers	Richard	32	9 Mount	
	Ann	32	"	
	Richard	3	"	
	Agnes	4	"	
	James	2	"	
	Thomas	1	"	
Huthersall	Elizabeth	60	7 Mount	
Haggers	Agnes	4	"	42
	Margeret	38	81 Fishergate	
Humphries	Martha	30	17 "	
Hurst	Ruth	59	Mount Pleasant	
	Mary	30	"	
	Thomas	21	"	
	Ellen	17	"	
	Ann	14	"	
	Ruth	9	"	
	Nancy	1	"	
Hardicar	Debora	22	3 Well	
Hall	Ann	53	10 Heatley	
	Betty	14	"	
Halliwell	Richard	18	20 "	
Harrison	Betsy	46	5 Simpson	
	Mary	15	"	
	Ann	9	"	
Harrison	Nancy	28	"	
Holmes	Ellen	29	35 Friargate	
Hodgson	Isabella	70	36 "	

1820 Census — Catholic Congregation of Preston

Surname	Forename(s)	Age	Address	Comm
Hargreaves	Winifrid		35 [Friargate]	
	Ann		"	
Heyes	Catherine		"	
Higginson	Mary	54	13 Hill	
	Ann	15	"	
Holmes	Joseph	29	5 Snowhill	
	Jane	27	"	
	John	2	"	
	Catherine	1	"	
	Sarah	1	"	
Houghton	William	27	134 Friargate	
	Jane	23	"	
	Ellen	5	"	
	Mary	3	"	
	John	2	"	
Haggars	Richard	65	"	
	William	25	"	
Hoyle	Elisabeth	60	Warings Yard	
	Jane	32	"	
	Dorothy	24	"	
	Hannah	18	"	
	Richard	10	"	
Holmes	Robert	74	55 Friargate	
	Elizabeth	77	"	
Hall	William	45	58 "	
	Ellen	46	"	
	James	20	"	
	Jane	18	"	
	Ann	16	"	
	Catherine	15	"	
	Mary	12	"	
	William	1	"	
Howarth	Mary	53	79 Friargate	
	Margt	15	"	
	John	11	"	
Higginson	James	22	97 "	
	Jane	1	"	
Hodgkinson	John	54	120 "	
	Elizabeth	49	"	
	Catherine	20	"	
	Cicily	19	"	
	William	11	"	
	Ann	9	"	
Hoyles	Winifrid	65	121 "	
	Joshua	28	"	
Hall	William	33	33 Vauxhall Road	
	Dorothy	31	"	
Hargreaves	Catherine		27 "	
Hodson	John		Oak	
	Mary		"	

1820 Census   Catholic Congregation of Preston

Surname	Forename(s)	Age	Address	Comm
[Hodson]	Thomas	18	[Oak]	
	Joseph	16	"	
	Mary	16	"	
	Betty	15	"	
	John	10	"	
	Margt	8	"	
	Robert	6	"	
	James	3	"	
	William	1	"	
Harrison	Thomas		20 Vauxhall	
	Betty		"	
Holyday	William		"	
	Alice		"	
	Mary	3	"	
	Betty	1	"	
Harrison	Margt		Charlotte	
	Thomas	18	"	
	Dorothy	17	"	
	Nancy	15	"	
	Aggy	13	"	
	John	11	"	
	Betty	7	"	
	Mary	4	"	
	Jane	1	"	
Holland	Patrick		7 Back Charlotte	
	Henrietta		"	
	John	5	"	
	William	2	"	
	Elizabeth	1	"	
Holderness	William		8 Back Charlotte	
Harrison	James		"	
	Ann		"	
	John	18	"	
	Mary	15	"	
	Edward	10	"	
	James	7	"	
	Lawrence	2	"	
Holderness	John		5 "	
	Alice		"	
	Margeret		"	
	Ann	19	"	
	Peter	19	"	
	Betty	18	"	
	Mary	17	"	
	Margt	15	"	
	John	13	"	
Hartley	Elizabeth		28 "	
Holderness	George		"	
	William	9	"	
	Mary	6	"	

1820 Census   Catholic Congregation of Preston

Surname	Forename(s)	Age	Address	Comm
[Holderness]	George	4	[Back Charlotte]	
	James	1	"	
Holywell	William		"	
	Ellen		"	
	John	6	"	
	Joseph	3	"	
	William	1	"	
Harrison	Abraham		"	
	Grace		"	
	Betty	14	"	
	Abraham	13	"	
Hall	Easter		Bk King	
Harley	Lawrence		"	
	Jane		"	
	Ann	15	"	
	Mary	12	"	
	John	8	"	
	William	7	"	
	Betty	3	"	
	James	1	"	
Holderness	George		William	
	Mary		"	
	Mary	4	"	
	John	1	"	
	William		"	
Heves	Richard		Paradise	
	Mary		"	
	Oswall	16	"	
	Agnes	14	"	
	Ann	12	"	
	Richard	9	"	
Helm	Thomas		Paradise	
	Betty		"	
	Dorothy	7	"	
	Robert	3	"	
	Teresa	1	"	
Hodson	Richard	8	28 Back Queen St	
	William	2	"	
	Robert	4	"	
	Alice		"	
Holmes	Mathew		27 "	
	Grace		"	
	Thomas	19	"	
	Dorothy	18	"	
	Mathew	1	"	
Herst	Ann		"	
Harrison	John		24 "	
	Jane		"	
Hardman	Peter		28 Queen	
	Mary		"	

1820 Census   Catholic Congregation of Preston

Surname	Forename(s)	Age	Address	Comm
[Hardman]	Betty		[Queen]	
	John	21	"	
	Thomas	18	"	
	Ann	17	"	
	Betty	15	"	
	Alice	12	"	
	James	11	"	
	Bella	10	"	
	Peter	8	"	
	Jane	5	"	
	Ellen	3	"	
	Mary	?6	"	
Hodson	Margt		Willow	
	Nancy	14	"	
	Dorothy	9	"	
Hayes	Ann		4 King	
	Mageret	18	"	
	Sarah	11	"	
Hartley	John	13	"	
	Ellen		"	
	Richard	5	"	
	William	3	"	
	Mary Ann	1	"	
Helman	Betty		Park St	
Hollinhurst	Richd		21 King	
	Eliza		"	
	Susannah		"	
	Margt	2	"	
Heaton	Thomas	30	"	
	Hetty	20	"	
Hornby	William		Paradise	
	Francis		"	
	Eliza	11	"	
Holderness	George		37 Singleton Row	
	Mary		"	
	James	1	"	
Hodson	Robert		4 Harrison Hill	
	John	25	"	
	James	23	"	
	Thomas	21	"	
	Anthony	20	"	
	Mathew	18	"	
	Henry	16	"	
	Thomas	14	"	
	Richard	13	"	
	Robert	9	"	
	Isabella	7	"	
	Charles	6	"	
Heaton	James		15 Singletons Row	
Harrison	John		6 Craggs Court	

1820 Census　　　Catholic Congregation of Preston

Surname	Forename(s)	Age	Address	Comm
[Harrison]	Margt		[Craggs Court]	
	Maria	17	"	
	Ellen	15	"	
	Edward	13	"	
	Joseph	10	"	
	Betty	9	"	
	Easter	6	"	
Hoskinson	Michael	8	"	
	Mary	2	"	
Helmon	Jane			
Harrison	Thomas		3 North St	
	Mary		"	
	Margt	4	"	
	Ellen	2	"	
	James	1	"	
Hosberndeston	George		Crows	
	Alice		"	
	John	6	"	
	James	4	"	
	Joseph	2	"	
	George	1	"	
Halfpenny	James			
Helman	James		12 Singletons row	
	Mary		"	
	John	12	"	
	Ann	11	"	
	Margt	5	"	
	Alice	3	"	
	Maria	1	"	
Hornby	Ellen	40	30 Dale Street	
Hardman	Richard	42	1 Holdens Square	
	Margt	41	"	
	John	21	"	
	Margt	16	"	
	James	14	"	
	William	12	"	
	Richard	10	"	
	Lawrence	7	"	
	Thomas	4	"	
Holden	Henry	37	10 "	
	Mary	38	"	
	Eliza	16	"	
	John	14	"	
	Robert	12	"	
	James	10	"	
	Margt	8	"	
	Ellen	6	"	
	Henry	4	"	
	Jane	1	"	
Helme	John	45	15 "	

1820 Census   Catholic Congregation of Preston

Surname	Forename(s)	Age	Address	Comm
[Helme]	Nancy	46	[Holdens Square]	
	William	22	"	
	James	25	"	
	Eliza	15	"	
Helme	Nancy	28	28 "	
	Margt	14	"	
Hall	Lawrence	26	Moorside	
	Ann		"	
Hall	John		"	
	Ellen		"	
	James	8	"	
	Henry	6	"	
	Ann	4	"	
	John	1	"	
Hool	Bernard	46	44 Canal Street	
	Alice	46	"	
	Joseph	11	"	
	George	9	"	
	Barnaby	6	"	
	Richard	4	"	
Higginson	James	34	42 "	
Hull	Mary	50	Canal Street	
	Thomas	38	"	
Hall	Ellen	40	40 "	
	Robert	22	"	
	Ellen	21	"	
	Ann	16	"	
	Margt	11	"	
	John	8	"	
Haydock	George	38	26 "	
	Thomas	16	"	
	William	14	"	
	Mary	11	"	
Holden	Richard	72	18 "	
	Richard	16	"	
	Henry	14	"	
Holden	Jane	27	18 "	
	Mary	8	"	
Holyday	John	36	18 "	
	Fanny	42	"	
	Margt	16	"	
	Ellen	14	"	
	Robert	12	"	
	Betty	8	"	
	Mary	2	"	
Holland	Joseph	21	15 Hope	
Houghton	Mary	87	16 "	
	Ann	8	"	
Hoodhear	William	60	Fosters Square	
	Elizabeth	34	"	

1820 Census   Catholic Congregation of Preston

Surname	Forename(s)	Age	Address	Comm
[Hoodhear]	Elizabeth	23	[Fosters Square]	
	Margeret	18	"	
Hallan	Margeret	80	"	
	Margeret	43		
	Margeret	22	"	
	John	3	"	
Hardman	James	60	"	
	Mary	49	"	
	James	11	"	
	Joseph	9	"	
Hogben	Thomas	25	Bk Canal	
	Jane	25	"	
	Mary	9	"	
	Ellin	2	"	
Hargreaves	Henry	40	1 Hope Street	
	Betty	48	"	
	Ellen	14	"	
	John	10	"	
	Agnes	7	"	
	William	3	"	
Hays	Thomas	23	"	
	Ann	3	"	
	Christr	1	"	
Huddersall	Jane	40	18 "	
	Thomas	11	"	
	Richard	8	"	
	Ann	5	"	
Holding	Henry	37	Bridge	
	Mary	34	"	
	Joseph	17	"	
	Betty	14	"	
	Jane	10	"	
	Bella	1	"	
Hardman	John	32	"	
	Margt	32	"	
	Thomas	9	"	
	Ellin	8	"	
Hubbersty	Henry	58	25 "	
	Jane	70	"	
Horston	Agnes	50	39 "	
Hodgson	Thomas	28	16 Bridge St Lane	
	Catherine	25	"	
	James	4	"	
	Catherine	3	"	
	John	2	"	
	Mary	1	"	
Holgate	Matthew	23	12 "	
	Catherine	27	"	
	Gabriel	3	"	
	Ann	1	"	

1820 Census   Catholic Congregation of Preston

Surname	Forename(s)	Age	Address	Comm
Hothersall	John	52	4 Sopery	
	Margt	51	"	
	Henry	23	"	
	John	20	"	
	Margt	15	"	
	Nancy	14	"	
Harrison	Jane	56	15 Sopery	
	Mary	30	"	
	James	11	"	
	Thomas	7	"	
Hubbersty	Robert		Friday St	
	Jane		"	
	Betty	8	"	
	Bella	5	"	
	William	3	"	
Holding	Ann		"	
	James	21	"	
Holyday	George	64	73 Bk Lane	
	Betty	60	"	
Horracks	Fracis	22	11 Friargate	43
Hornby	Jane	26	"	
	Thomas	12	"	
Hodson	Elizabeth	19	24 "	
Hays	James	59	Shambles	
	Elizabeth	59	"	
Howard	Dorothy	34	Molyneux Square	
	John	7	"	
	Elizabeth	3	"	
Hubbersty	William	19	18 Shambles	
Hubbersty	Thomas	34	3 Market Place	
Huthersall	Ann	25	42 "	
	Ellen	14	"	
Hindle	Bella	23	28 Lune	
Hool	Mary	15	176 Friargate	
Howarth	Mary		20 Pleasant	
Hodkinson	L		Sike Hill	
Hall	Betty		Turks head yard	
	Lawrence	2	"	
Hayran	James	30	Library	
Hulme	Alice		Rose	
	John		"	
	John	5	"	
	Jane	1	"	
Hall	Thomas	15	10 "	
Holding	John		"	
	Mary	1?	"	
	Agnes	11	"	
	John	9	"	
	James	7	"	
Houghton	Sally	64	27 High Street	

1820 Census — Catholic Congregation of Preston

Surname	Forename(s)	Age	Address	Comm
[Houghton]	Mary	41	[High Street]	
	Betty	16	"	
	Sally	31	"	
	George	10	"	
	Thomas	3	"	
Houghton	Edward	38	28 "	
	Ellen	40	"	
	William	18	"	
	John	14	"	
	Thomas	12	"	
	Sally	10	"	
	Richard	7	"	
	Charles	5	"	
	Edward	3	"	
	James	1	"	
Horrax	Mr		Everton Gardens	
	Mrs		"	
	Dorothy	1	"	
Holmes	Betty	65	20 Whitakers row	
	Mary	18	"	
Hoggen	Betty	30	18 "	
Hodgson	Jane	22	22 Bk Kirkham	
	Jona	1	"	
Hull	Matthew	55	18 Kirkham	
	Betty	56	"	
	Margt	22	"	
	Robert	19	"	
	Christr	9	"	
	Betty	5	"	
	Eliza	1	"	
Hardman	William	39	10 Cold Bath St	
	Mary	42	"	
	Bridget	19	"	
	Robert	17	"	
Holmes	Joseph	29	"	
	Jane	27	"	
	John	2	"	
	Catherine	1	"	
	Sarah	4m	"	
Higgins	Patrick	50	38 Snow hill	
	Margt	19	"	
	Agnes	14	"	
	John	11	"	
Higginson	William	37	32 Vicar	
	Helen	48	"	
	William	15	"	
	Sarah	11	"	
	Ralph	8	"	
	Richard	6	"	
	Robert	3	"	

1820 Census   Catholic Congregation of Preston

Surname	Forename(s)	Age	Address	Comm
Hunter	Ann	39	[Vicar]	
	William		"	
	James	11	"	
Houghton	Margeret	42	8 "	
Holding	Richard	26	18 Walker	
	Ann	31	"	
Hool	William	22	27 "	
	Ann	24	"	
	John	1	"	
Holding	John	23	18 Walker	
Helme	Richard	34	Ribbleton	
	Richard	68	"	
	Grace	61	"	
	Joseph	41	"	
Hodkinson	Rose	59	Marsh	
	Alice	4	"	
Hodgson	John	22	Ashton Brows	
Higginson	Ann	20	Long Lane	
Hodson	Thomas	14	Nr Tulketh Hall	
Hill	John	28	Water lane end	
	Rachel	26	"	
	William	4	"	
	James	2	"	
	Ellen	1	"	
Hubbersty	John		Fulwood	
	Alice		"	
	Ellen		"	
	Thomas		"	
Horn	Thomas		Fulwood	
	Ann		"	
	Thomas		"	
	John		"	
	Ann		"	
	Joseph		"	
	Mary		"	
Hool	Joseph		"	
Hubbersty	James		"	
	Mary		"	
	Peggy		"	
	Peggy		"	
Hodson	Elizabeth		"	
Helm	George		"	
	Mary		"	
	George		"	
	Ann		"	
	Jane		"	
Jackson	William	40	119 Church St	
	Betty	45	"	
	Ann	13	"	
	John	11	"	

1820 Census   Catholic Congregation of Preston

Surname	Forename(s)	Age	Address	Comm
[Jackson]	Mary	8	[Church St]	
	William	4	"	
Ibbitt	Nathan	70	11 Holdens yard	
	Ann	57	"	
	Ann	21	"	
Jackson	George		56 Fishergate	
Johnson	Mary		59 West end	
Jones	Sarah	?24	12 Cannon	44
Just	Vincent	40	7 Hill	
	Alice	45	"	
	Ann	14	"	
	Lucy	9	"	
Ireland	Sally	30	55 Friargate	
Jamieson	John	41	Prescotts yard	
	Ellen	38	"	
Jones	Ellen		Charlotte	
	William		"	
Jones	Ellen		William	
Jolly	Ann		William	
Johnson	John		9 Water	
	Mary		"	
	Grace	10	"	
	Jessia	8	"	
	Mark	3	"	
	Thomas	1	"	
Jackson	Betty	53	9 Bridge St Lane	
	John	25	"	
	Catherine	13	"	
	Betty	23	"	
	Betty	5	"	
	William	1	"	
Jenkinson	Betty		Friday	
	Ann	1	"	
Idle	Thomas	17	11 Friargate	
Johnson	Alice		Pleasant St	
	Margeret		"	
	John		"	
	Mary Ann	10	"	
	Robert	13	"	
	Alexander	16	"	
Jenkinson	Ann	27	1 Fable St	
	James	3	"	
	John	2	"	
Jackson	Ann	25	29 Vicar Street	
	Helen		"	
Jackson	Thomas		Fulwood	
	Easter		"	
	Matthew		"	
	Thomas		"	
	James		"	

1820 Census Catholic Congregation of Preston

Surname	Forename(s)	Age	Address	Comm
[Jackson]	Betty		[Fulwood]	
	Alice		"	
	Mary		"	
	Ellen		"	
	Bella		"	
Johnson	Sarah		"	
	Mary		"	
	Ellen		"	
	Betty		"	
	Sarah		"	
Johnson	Frank		"	
	Ann		"	
	James		"	
	Robert		"	
	John		"	
	Betty		"	
	Richard		"	
Kellatt	Jenny	66	7 St John St	
Kay	Joseph	32	8 Cotton Court	
	Winifrid	33	"	
	Mary	1	"	
Kay	George	41	15 Mount	
	Ann	32	"	
	Elizabeth	13	"	
	Agnes	12	"	
	Isabella	11	"	
	Ann	9	"	
	William	7	"	
	John	5	"	
	James	3	"	
Kellatt	Robert	65	5 "	
	Elizabeth	55	"	
	Ann	21	"	
Kitching	Henry	30	18 Heatley	
	Betty	34	"	
	Mary	10	"	
	Margeret	8	"	
	Ellen	5	"	
	Jane	3	"	
	Isabella	1	"	
Kitching	Henry	62	36 Friargate	
	Jane	60	"	
	Mary	3	"	
Kitchin	Joseph		5 Leeming	
	Henry		"	
Kenyon	Joseph		4 King	
	Elizabeth		"	
	Ellen	9	"	
	Christ	6	"	
	Cicely	4	"	

1820 Census   Catholic Congregation of Preston

Surname	Forename(s)	Age	Address	Comm
[Kenyon]	Ann	2	[King]	
Kilshaw	Jane		Paradise	
Kay	John		Singletons Row	
	Ellen		"	
	Peter	30	"	
	Andrew	19	"	
	John	11	"	
	Wardley	4	"	
Kellett	Thomas	33	"	
	Betty		"	
	Ellen	1	"	
Kay	Ann	39	1 Kirkham	
	Susanna	16	"	
	Maria	4	"	
Kinson	James	34	4 Bengal Square	
	Alice	33	"	
	Alice	13	"	
	Mary	11	"	
	William	14	"	
Kelly	Michal	32	1 Hope	
	Ann	40	"	
Kellat	Thomas			
Kitching	John		Library St	
	Ann		"	
	Mary Ann	12	"	
	William	10	"	
Kellat	Ann	2	Avenham	
Kay	Richard	57	9 Snow hill	
	Ellen	74	"	
	Margt	25	"	
	Alice		"	
Kellat	Robert	29	Greavestown	
	Mary	35	"	
	Betsy	5	"	
	John	3	"	
	Mary	1	"	
	Robert	28	"	
	Mary	16	"	
Leach	Nancy	41	Germans yard	
	Peggy	13	"	
Leigh	Peter	86	Dixons yard	
Leeming	Bridget	18	8 Church	
Loftnouse	Elizabeth	69	6 Cock yard	
	James	30	"	
Lawson	Isabella	46	27 Fishergate	
	William	15	"	
	John	12	"	
Langdale	Ellen	50	3 Theatre	
	Fanny	23	"	
Lyon	Margeret	19	1 Lune	

1820 Census   Catholic Congregation of Preston

Surname	Forename(s)	Age	Address	Comm
Lomax	John	18	Chapel	
Leeming	George	34	5 Simpson	
	Alice	29	"	
	Mary	6	"	
Latus	Isabella	7	1 Ratcliff	
Lawson	John	35	3 Hill	
	Agnes	26	"	
	Jane	15	"	
	James	12	"	
	Mary	8	"	
	William	2	"	
	Joseph	1	"	
Lawrenson	Betty	5	4 "	
Lancaster	Mary		10 Vauxhall	
	Catherine		"	
Leigh	William		Park St	
	Margeret		"	
	John	10	"	
	Peter	6	"	
Levesey	John		Charlotte	
	Betty		"	
	Betty	18	"	
	William	13	"	
Layfield	-		Walton	
Lupton	Joseph		"	
	Elizabeth		"	
	Joseph	8	"	
	Elizabeth	6	"	
	William	4	"	
	Mary	2	"	
Lancaster	Mary		Paradise	
Lee	Thomas		24 Queen	
	Mary		"	
	David		"	
	James	19	"	
	Michael	17	"	
	John	10	"	
	Ellen	3	"	
	Alice	3	22 "	
	Peter		22 "	
	Mary	1	22 "	
Latus	James	42	42 Singleton's Row	
	Isabella	42	"	
	Grace	18	"	
	John	16	"	
	Richard	15	"	
	Robert	13	"	
	Ellen	11	"	
	George	9	"	
	Mary	7	"	

1820 Census   Catholic Congregation of Preston

Surname	Forename(s)	Age	Address	Comm
[Latus]	Agnes	5	[Singleton's Row]	
	Ann	3	"	
	Isabella	1	"	
Lee	Thomas	23	"	
	Margt		"	
	Betty	2	"	
	William	1	"	
Leeming	Richard		North St	
	Ellen		"	
Leach	John		"	
	Agnes		"	
	William	16	"	
	Margt	15	"	
	Easter	14	"	
	John	12	"	
	Dorothy	10	"	
Langtree	Grace		Crows	
Livesey	William	60	36 Dale	
	Ellen	59	"	
	Mary	36	"	
	Eliza	32	"	
	Ann	29	"	
	Joseph	20	"	
	John	17	"	
	Peter	13	"	
Livesey	Thomas	31	10 Stanley	
	Eliza	34	"	
	Ellen	7	"	
	William	5	"	
	Maria	1	"	
Lawrence	Lawrence	36	5 Green	
	Elizabeth	37	"	
	Nancy	13	"	
	Rachel	5	"	
Leach	Joseph	22	4 Moorside	
Latham	Nancy	63	42 Canal	
Lupton	Thomas	50	"	
Leach	William	44	11 Canal	
	Ann	53	"	
	James	22	"	
	Margt	21	"	
	John	19	"	
	Ellen	16	"	
	Charles	14	"	
	Richard	12	"	
	Thomas	10	"	
Livesey	Dorothy	26	3 Hope	
	George	5	"	
	Ann	2	"	
	Margt	1	"	

1820 Census **Catholic Congregation of Preston**

Surname	Forename(s)	Age	Address	Comm
Leeming	Thomas	21	3 [Hope]	
	Bella	21	"	
	Jane	1	"	
Leeming	Mathew	18	3 "	
Lunn	Thomas	28	Bridge	
	Jane	28	"	
	James	1	"	
Leach	James	53	34 "	
	Sarah	49	"	
	William	25	"	
	James	18	"	
	John	15	"	
	Mary	13	"	
	Margt	8	"	
	Richard	6	"	
Latus	Mary	54	37 "	
Lawrenson	John	46	9 "	
	Agnes	42	"	
	Jane	18		
	Mary	17	"	
	John	10	"	
	Robert	6	"	
	Betty	3	"	
	Agnes	1	"	
Latus	Ellen	11	11 "	
Lancaster	George	55	12 "	45
	Margt	49	"	
	Richard	17	"	46
	Betty	15	"	
	Lucy	13	"	
	Agnes	11	"	
	George	8	"	
Lunn	Henry	40	14 Bridge St	
	Margt	65	"	
	Betty	40	"	
Lever	John	49	13 Sopery	
	Sarah	48	"	
	Jane	24	"	
	Robert	17	"	
	Obediah	17	"	
	Alice	13	"	
	Jane	9	"	
	Joseph	9	"	
Livesey	Ann		15 Shambles	
Livisey	Michael	47	Molyneux Square	
	Nancy	57	"	
Lambert	Richard	19	Wards end	
Leach	Betty	43	Friargate	
	Margt	21	"	
	Nancy	19	"	

1820 Census   Catholic Congregation of Preston

Surname	Forename(s)	Age	Address	Comm
[Leach]	Betty	15	[Friargate]	
	Lucy	13	"	
	William	26	"	
Lund	Elinor		"	
Leisay	William	50	"	
	Ann	37	"	
	John	7	"	
	Sarah	1	"	
Lawrenson	Mary		10 Rose	
Lodge	Eliza		Woodcock	
Layfield	Charles	52	54 High St	
	Jane	49	"	
Lantree	John	48	"	
	Margeret	30	"	
	John	1	"	
	Ann	78	"	
Lindelf	Sarah	34	Everton Gardens	
	Francis	11	"	
	Mary	6	"	
	Nancy	1		
Leach	James	30	28 Whitakers row	
Layland	Alice		27 Bk Kirkham	
	John	14	"	
	Lester	10	"	
	Hannah	8	"	
	Alice	4	"	
	Mary	1	"	
Livesey	Thomas	61	Vicars	47
Livesey	William	55	10 Walker	
	Jane	56	"	
	William	19	"	
Lawrenson	James	31	Ribbleton	
	Lucy	21	"	
	John	1	"	
Leeming	Joseph	34	Marsh end	
Lund	Anthony	39	Long Lane	
	Margt	36	"	
	John	12	"	
	Mary	10	"	
	Cuthbert	8	"	
	Robert	6	"	
	James	4	"	
	Anthony	2	"	
	William	1	"	
Lovet	James		Fulwood	
Livesey	Ann		"	
Markland	Robert	50	Park	
	Elizabeth	52	"	
Moon	John	24	22 Nile	
	Ellen	24	"	

133

1820 Census — Catholic Congregation of Preston

Surname	Forename(s)	Age	Address	Comm
[Moon]	Robert	3	[Nile]	
Myerscough	Rowland	27	12 Clarks yard	
	Jane	4	"	
	Betsy	2	"	
Marsh	John	39	4 Cotton Court	
	Mary	40	"	
	Ellen	13	"	
	Peggy	11	"	
	John	5	"	
Machell	William	67	3 Church	
	Ann	40	"	
	William	15	"	
	Betty	10	"	
	Catherine	7	"	
Marsh	Elizabeth	55	2 Butlers Court	
	Ellen	30	"	
Marshall	John		Fishergate Lane	
	Jane		"	
Middelton	-		West end	
Mason	Mary	24	69 Fishergate	
Machel	James	34	3 Fox	
	Mary	30	"	
	Leonard	5	"	
	George	3	"	
	Elizabeth	1	"	
Mason	Richard	42	23 Mount	
	Elizabeth	39	"	
	Jane	12	"	
	Richard	10	"	
	Mary	8	"	
	Helen	5	"	
	Alice	2	"	
	Ann	49	"	
Macneal	Isabella	50	113 Fishergate	
Miller	Luke	5	7 Chandler	
Mayor	Richard	38	13 Boran	
	Ann	28	"	
	Richard	10	"	
	Alice	5	"	
Myerscough Senr	John	71	15 Heatley	
	John	40	"	
	Mary	38	"	
	Nancy	15	"	
	Mary	13	"	
	Betsy	9	"	
	Ellen	7	"	
	Alice	5	"	
	Margeret	2	"	
	Ellen	42	"	
Melling	James	65	1 Ratcliff	

1820 Census — Catholic Congregation of Preston

Surname	Forename(s)	Age	Address	Comm
[Melling]	Margeret	70	[Ratcliff]	
Mutch	James	45	4 Hill	
	Ellen	49	"	
	Charles	15	"	
	Elizabeth	14	"	
	Jude	7	"	
	Ellen	3	"	
McGowan	Manasses	46	137 Friargate	
	Francis	15	"	
	John	10	"	
	Catherine	7		
Melling	Thomas	4	Lills yard	
Mather	James	50	Back Lane	
	Dorothy	53	"	
	Nicholas	5	"	
Mercer	James	43	"	
	Margeret	43	"	
	Silvester	17	"	
	James	15	"	
	John	13	"	
	Ellen	11	"	
	Elizabeth	4	"	
Miller	Catherine	32	"	
	John	8	"	
Mounsey	Mary	54		
Mills	Margt	27	Warings yard	
Mason	Elizabeth	54	52 Friargate	
Mayor	William	20	Vauxhall	
Morley	John		Park St	
	Mary		"	
	Thomas	15	"	
	Leddy	11	"	
	Mary	8	"	
	Ann	6	"	
	Alice	3	"	
	John	1	"	
Makin	Thomas		6 Charlotte	
	Margt		"	
	James	1	"	
Margison	Richard		"	
Massy	Jane		"	
Melling	Henry			
Melling	Miss		Walton	
Miller	Christopher		12 Leeming	
	Thomas		"	
	Ann		"	
	Mary		"	
Miller	Thomas	14	28 Back Queen St	
	Ellen		"	
Miller	Ellen	23	"	

1820 Census   Catholic Congregation of Preston

Surname	Forename(s)	Age	Address	Comm
Mighall	Richard		29 Queen	
	Mary		"	
	James		"	
	Ann		"	
	Catherine		"	
	Henry		"	
	Betty		"	
	Harriot		"	
	Richard	9	"	
	James	7	"	
Mailey	James		20 "	
	Sarah		"	
	Mary Ann	15	"	
Marley	Robert		8 Duke	
	Alice		"	
	Miles	17	"	
	Mary	15	"	
	James	13	"	
	Betty	10	"	
	Robert	4	"	
Morley	James		22 "	
	Mary		"	
	Betty	24	"	
	Peggy	22	"	
	William	20	"	
	Nancy	18	"	
	Mary	19	"	
	Mary	2	"	
	Nancy	1	"	
Morley	Betty		31 "	
	William	11	"	
	Mary	5	"	
	Alice	2	"	
Macral	Richard		29 King	
	Ellen		"	
	James	23	"	
	Mary Ann	16	"	
	Eliza	12	"	
	John	10	"	
	William	8	"	
	Ann	6	"	
Marsh	James		Paradise	
	Alice		"	
McConnel	Ann		13 Singletons Row	
Marsden	Ann		39 "	
Mullen	Nicholas		23 "	
McKenning	B		Crows	
	Ann		"	
	Mary	9	"	
	John	5	"	

1820 Census   Catholic Congregation of Preston

Surname	Forename(s)	Age	Address	Comm
[McKenning]	Rosanna	1	[Crows]	
McCowen	James		"	
Moss	Betty		"	
	Joseph	15	"	
	Jane	17	"	
	Margeret	10	"	
Moss	William		"	
	Jane		"	
	Ann	5	"	
	Betty	1	"	
March	Betty		"	
	Thomas		"	
	Lucy	2	"	
McLockeland	Daniel		"	
	Alice		"	
	James	5	"	
	Thomas	3	"	
	Daniel	2	"	
	William	1	"	
Moss	James		"	
Minto	Mary		"	
	George	9	"	
	Ann	7	"	
	Daniel	5	"	
	Jane	3	"	
	James	2	"	
	Mary	1	"	
Miller	Roger		"	
	Ellen		"	
	Alice	14	"	
	Ellen	12	"	
	Betty	9	"	
	Robert	6	"	
	Margeret	5	"	
	Ann	3	"	
	Mary	1	"	
Miller	John		Crows St	
	Margeret		"	
	Mary	16	"	
	Thomas	14	"	
	William	7	"	
	Ellen	5	"	
	Henry	2	"	
McMain	Margeret		"	
McWilliam	William		"	
	Susan			
McMain	James		3 Singletons row	
	John	18	"	
	Easter	16	"	
	Margt	10	"	

1820 Census   Catholic Congregation of Preston

Surname	Forename(s)	Age	Address	Comm
[McMain]	Sarah	8	[Singletons row]	
	Ann	6	"	
	Bridget	4	"	
McCanna	Francis	50	8 Ribbleton Lane	
	Rossy	48	"	
	John	24	"	
	Mary	14	"	
	Ellen	12	"	
	Rossy	8	"	
	Nancy	5	"	
Merris	Michal	36	12 "	
McTire	John	59	15 "	
	Margt	56	"	
	John	26	"	
	Charles	20	"	
	Ellen	17	"	
	Henry	14	"	
	Patrick	12	"	
Melling	Joseph	60	31 Stanley	
	Elizabeth	58	"	
	Richard	31	"	
	Thomas	28	"	
	Ellen	25	"	
Miller	John	18	"	
McCanna	John	38	12 Holden Square	
	Jane	39	"	
	Michal	16	"	
	Thomas	17	"	
	Sarah	6	"	
McCanna	Bernard	50	21 Holdens Square	
	Alice	47	"	
	Charles	21	"	
	Joseph	16	"	
	John	11	"	
	Bernard	9	"	
Mathew	Daniel	30	"	
	Eliza	28	"	
	John	4	"	
	Margt	2	"	
Moss	Margt	40	9 Bread	
	Thomas	19	"	
	Silvester	16	"	
	William	14		
	Alice	10	"	
	John	4	"	
Marginson	John	50	41 Canal	
	Dorothy	50	"	
	Dorothy	15	"	
	Rosella	10	"	
Murphy	Thomas	25	"	

1820 Census — Catholic Congregation of Preston

Surname	Forename(s)	Age	Address	Comm
[Murphy]	Catherine	23	[Canal]	
Murphy	Richard	39	"	
	Catherine	40	"	
	James	16	"	
Mason	Mary	40	Fosters square	
	Nancy	19	"	
	John	17	"	
	William	15	"	
	Joseph	3	"	
	Mary	1	"	
Moon	Nancy	28	Hope	
	Betty	6	"	
	Margt	5	"	
	John	3	"	
	Mary	1	"	
Melling	William	13	"	
	Susanna	20	"	
	Ellen	22	"	
March	Thomas	84	Bridge	
	Lucy	84	"	
	Jane	50	"	
	Betty	40	"	
Masow	Nancy	28	24 Bridge	
	Nancy	10	"	
	John	8	"	
	Jane	3	"	
	Richard	1	"	
Melling	Sussan	18	5 Anchor Wiend	
Melling	Joseph	44	26 Friargate	
	Alice	40	"	
Mally	Ellen	22	11 Shambles	
McCasto	Hugh	33	"	
	Margt	28	"	
	Charles	3	"	
McNally	William	34	Waterworths yard	
	Edward	12	"	
	Rosana	10	"	
	Samuel	8	"	
	Mary	5	"	
Moxom	Ellen	22	5 Gin Bow Entry	
Mayor	Margeret	40	30 Lune	
	Mary	19	"	
	P	29	"	
Moor	Thomas		151 Friargate	
	Mrs		"	
Mercer	Dorothy	19	"	
Molyneux	Eli	31	164 "	
	Ann	3	"	
	Thomas	1	"	
Macoin	John	46	"	

1820 Census   Catholic Congregation of Preston

Surname	Forename(s)	Age	Address	Comm
[Macoin]	Ann	53	[Friargate]	
McKenzie	Mr		41 Pleasant	
Marlow	Dorothy		Sike Hill	
	Nancy		"	
	Betty	18	"	
	Robert	16	"	
	Matthew	13	"	
	Ann	9	"	
Melling	James		Bostock St	
	Thomas	13	"	
	William	10	"	
	John	10	"	
	William	40	"	
Metcalf	Francis		Stonygate	
Martin	John		"	
Moon	John		5 Library	
Marlow	James		Rose	
	Betty		"	
	John	8	"	
	Matthew	2	"	
Marlow	William		57 Pleasant	
	Eliza		"	
	Mary	5	"	
	Robert	2	"	
Mallin	James	76	36 High	
	Dorothy	76	"	
Mahon	William	9	"	48
Metcalf	Betty	28	30 Whitakers row	
McCann	John	40	6 Tythe Barn	
McNeese	Margt	30	5 Kirkham	
	Edward	50	"	
	John	14	"	
	George	12	"	
	James	10	"	
	Joseph	7	"	
	Stephen	3	"	
Marsden	John	59	29 Bolton St	
	Betty	58	"	
	Betty	28	"	
	Ellen	26	"	
	Robert	15	"	
	Ann	12	"	
Maclure	James	22	Vicar	
	Mary	18	"	
	Daniel	1	"	
Meliing	Henry	40	"	
	Catherine	38	"	
	Ann	15	"	
	Jane	11	"	
	James	9	"	

1820 Census   Catholic Congregation of Preston

Surname	Forename(s)	Age	Address	Comm
[Meiling]	Betty	7	[Vicar]	
	Maria	7	"	
	Harriot		"	
Melling	Elizabeth	30	Bk Vicar Street	
Miller	John	17	Ribbleton	
Miller	Thomas	48	Marsh end	
	Nancy	45	"	
	Thomas	16	"	
	James	9	"	
	Francis	7	"	
Mather	James		Fulwood	
	Thomas		"	
	Bella		"	
	Margt		"	
Miller	Mary		"	
	Ann		"	
	Jane		"	
	Thomas		"	
	John		"	
Moss	John		"	
	Betty		"	
	John		"	
	Robert		"	
	James		"	
Miller	Robert		"	
	Dorothy		"	
Melling	John		"	
	Ann		"	
	Mary		"	
Mader	Thomas		"	
	Ann		"	
	John		"	
	Peter		"	
	Robert		"	
	Mary		"	
Miller	Ellen		"	
	John		"	
	Robert		"	
	Mary		"	
	Roger		"	
	James		"	
Moss	Thomas		"	
	Ellen		"	
Moss	Ellen		"	
Morris	James		"	
	Mary		"	
	Charles		"	
	Jane		"	
Miller	William		Fulwood	
	Ann		"	

1820 Census   Catholic Congregation of Preston

Surname	Forename(s)	Age	Address	Comm
[Miller]	Henry		[Fulwood]	
	Robert		"	
	John		"	
	Betty		"	
Moulding	Edward		"	
	Mary		"	
	Mary		"	
Noblet	Ann	18	41 Fishergate	
Norris	James	50	35 Mount	
	Ann	51	"	
	Ruth	10	"	
Nailor	Thomas	82	7 "	
Newsham	James	74	end of Chapel St	
	Thomas	41	"	
	Agnes	38	"	
	Frances	7	"	
Newby	Peter		4 Hill	
Nangles	Edward	52	43 Friargate	
	Jane	55	"	
	Ann	26	"	
	James	22	"	
	Ellin	20	"	
Nixon	Richard	29	137 "	
	Mary	30	"	
Nixon	Robert	41	113 "	
	Susan	31	"	
	James	4	"	
	Mary Ann	1	"	
Newsham	Thomas		27 Vauxhall	
Neale	Ann	10	10 "	
	William	14		
	John	13		
Noblett	Thomas		Harrison Hill	
	Rebecca		"	
	Richard	8	"	
	Grace	4	"	
	Alice	3	"	
	Betty	2	"	
	Thomas	1	"	
Nixon	Christopher	28	5 Canal	
	Ellin	32	"	
	Alice	12	"	
	John	9	"	
	Joseph	6	"	
	James	3	"	
	Charles	1	"	
Noblet	Richard	33	"	
	Nancy	33	"	
	Nancy	7	"	
	Thomas	4	"	

1820 Census Catholic Congregation of Preston

Surname	Forename(s)	Age	Address	Comm
[Noblet]	Joshua	2	[Canal]	
Noblet	James	26	16 "	
	Margt	25	"	
	John	6	"	
	Sarah	3	"	
Nixon	Joseph	72	14 Bridge	
Nobles	John		Field road	
	Margery		"	
	Agnes	1	"	
Noble	Edward		Bk Lane	
	John	17	"	
	Isabella	14	"	
	Daniel	11	"	
	Mary	9	"	
	Martin	3	"	
Naylor	Mrs		Library St	
	Lucy?		"	
Nightingale	John	12	Avenham	
Nick	William		44 High	
Osbaldeston	Joseph	54	7 Cotton Court	
	Ann	53	"	
	Margeret	30	"	
	Nancy	19	"	
	Esabella	18	"	
	Betty	14	"	
	Catherine	12	"	
	Joseph	9	"	
	Lucy	3	"	
Orrell	John	45	Friargate	
	Dorothy	45	"	
	James	23	"	
	Joseph	18	"	
	Jane	16	"	
	Ann	12	"	
	Dorothy	6	"	
Oldham	Thomas	18	12 King	
O Bryan	Francis		Crown	
	Mary		"	
	Ellen	7	"	
	Catherine	1	"	
O Bryan	Matthew		50 Singletons Row	
O Lack	Joseph	22	4 Moorside	49
O Coope	Joseph	32	"	50
	Ann	30	"	
	Mary	9	"	
	John	6	"	
	Joseph	4	"	
	Ann	2	"	
	Agnes	1	"	
Obin	Thomas	61	Ansons Square	

1820 Census   Catholic Congregation of Preston

Surname	Forename(s)	Age	Address	Comm
[Obin]	Margaret	58	[Ansons Square]	
	Betty	32	"	
	James	21	"	
	Agnes	18	"	
	Robert	14	"	
Osburn	Bernard		Stonygate	
Orrel	John	42	27 Friargate	
	Margeret	33	"	
	Mary	8	"	
	Ann	6	"	
	Ellen	4	"	
	Alice	2	"	
Oleary	Arthur	24	9 Fable St	
	Ann	2	"	
	Richard	1	"	
	Mary	20	"	
Owen	Michal	60	15 Kirkham	
	Ann	54	"	
	Michal	19	"	
	William	15	"	
	Catherine	13	"	
	James	12	"	
	Thomas	10	"	
	Ann	6	"	
Osbaldeston	John	51	21 Snow hill	
	Ann	48	"	
	William	12	"	
	James	11	"	
	Peter	7	"	
	Mary	3	"	
Preston	Richard	22	22 Nile Street	
Pilkinton	Mary	19	8 Church	
Parker	Henry	58	32 Mince Between	
	Alice	57	"	
	James	22	"	
	Jane	8	"	
Postlewhite	Margeret	45	15 Lills Yard	
	George	12	"	
	Ralph	9	"	
	Ann	10	"	
	Mary	6	"	
	Margeret	4	"	
Patrick	John	58	3 Church	
	Margaret	60	"	
Preston	Sarah	30	2 Willow Place	
Parkinson	Alice		West end	
Parkinson	Robert	23	69 Fishergate	
Pilkington	John	45	7 St Wilfrid	
	Elizabeth	39	"	
	William	12	"	

144

1820 Census Catholic Congregation of Preston

Surname	Forename(s)	Age	Address	Comm
[Pilkinton]	Ellen	10	[St Wilfrid]	
	Hugh	8	"	
	John	6	"	
	Thomas	5	"	
	Henry	3	"	
Parker	John	52	Fox	
	Jane	57	"	
Platt	Alice	36	111 Fishergate	
	Helen	12	"	
Pooles	James	30	32 Mount	
	Ann	40	"	
Proctor	Evan	27	20 "	
Proctor	James	59	16 "	
	Mary	50	"	
	Mary	19	"	
	Mary	9	"	
Parkinson	Margeret	32	11 "	
Proctor	George	62	4 Talbot	
Park	Thomas	42	Nr Canal Warehouse	
	Elizabeth	42	"	
Prescott	Robert	34	11 Hill	
	Ann	14	"	
	David	10	"	
	Jane	8	"	
	Mary	6	"	
	Agnes	4	"	
Pooles	James	22	97 Friargate	
	Elizabeth	24	"	
	Ann	1	"	
	Catherine	1	"	
Pye	Margt	24	113 "	
Pilling	Miss		Walton	
Proctor	James		10 Vauxhall	
	Nancy		"	
	Catherine	14	"	
	Mary	11	"	
	Alice	8	"	
	John	4	"	
	William	2	"	
Parkins	John		King	
	Ann		"	
	William	8	"	
	Robert	5	"	
Parkinson	Robt		10 Queen	
	Mary		"	
	Ann	16	"	
	Richard	11	"	
	Mary	3	"	
	Thomas	1	"	
Perkin	John		28 King	

1820 Census   Catholic Congregation of Preston

Surname	Forename(s)	Age	Address	Comm
[Perkin]	Ann		[King]	
	Robert	5	"	
	William	8	"	
Parkinson	Betty		Paradise	
Pickering	Father		Singleton Row	51
	Mother		"	
	Jane	5	"	
	John	2	"	
Proctor	Jane		4 Craggs row	
	Thomas		"	
Proctor	Ralph		2 Corry Street	
	Ann		"	
	Alice	15	"	
	Ralph	13	"	
	Mary	11	"	
	Betty	9	"	
	William	4	"	
Proctor	Ralph		"	
	Alice		"	
Piet	Alice	73	3 Crown	
Poulton	Mary		Craggs	
Philipcoft	Ann		North	
	Ann	20	"	
Parkson	John	32	7 Stanley	
	Eliza	34	"	
	Nancy	11	"	
	Maria	8	"	
	Matthew	2	"	
Parkson	Jane	40	10 Bengal Square	
	Joseph	19	"	
	James	17	"	
	Robert	14	"	
	Ralph	11	"	
Parkson	John	30	12 "	
	Jane	26	"	
	Ann	2	"	
Parkson	John	26	14 "	
	Ann	27	"	
	Diana	5	"	
	John	2	"	
Parkinson	William	41	Canal	
	Alice	38	"	
	Mary	19	"	
	Ann	15	"	
	Thomas	12	"	
	Jane	8	"	
	Alice	7	"	
	Margt	5	"	
	Hannah	3	"	
	Ellin	1	"	

1820 Census — Catholic Congregation of Preston

Surname	Forename(s)	Age	Address	Comm
Park	Mathew	55	35 Bridge	
	Ellen	48	"	
	James	23	"	
	Joseph	15	"	
	Mary	14	"	
	Robert	10	"	
	Ann	7	"	
	Martin	10	"	
Parkinson	James	38	10 Bridge St Lane	
	Ann	39	"	
	Ann	71	"	
	Thomas	17	"	
Parkinson	Thomas	61	17 "	
	Jane	50	"	
	Betty	18	"	
	Betty	12	"	
	Mary	10	"	
Parkinson	Margeret	22	11 Spring	
	Richard	24	"	
	Mary	19	"	
	John	22	10 "	
	Alice	21	"	
	Rob	1	"	
Parkinson	James	55	8 Friargate	
	Eliza	54	"	
	John	27	"	
	Mary	20	"	
	James	17	"	
	Ann	15	"	
	Eliza	13	"	
	William	12	"	
Pemberton	Rd	35	16 "	
	Elizabeth	34	"	
	William	10	"	
	Thomas	8	"	
	Ann	7	"	
	Jane	5	"	
	George	1	"	
Parkinson	Margt	65	14 Hardmans yard	
Paily	Catherine	51	24 Friargate	
	Ann	15	"	
Pickup	Ann	57	Molyneux Square	
	Ann	4	"	
Pemberton	Wm	60	4 Gin Bow entry	
Parker	John	25	Watermans Yard	52
	Betty	21	"	
	Ann	2	"	
Parkinson	John	20	27 Friargate	
Parkinson	Thomas	37	"	
	Ellen	37	"	

1820 Census   Catholic Congregation of Preston

Surname	Forename(s)	Age	Address	Comm
[Parkinson]	Sarah	11	[Friargate]	
	Betty	10	"	
	William	6	"	
	Ann	3	"	
	Margeret	1	"	
Palmer	Ellen		12 Bk Pleasant St	
Parker	James	37	105 High	
	Ann	35	"	
	Christopher	14	"	
	Richard	11	"	
	William	5	"	
	John	4	"	
	Catherine	2	"	
Preston	Robert	27	"	
	Alice	25	"	
	Robert	3	"	
	Ann	16	"	
Proctor	Betty	58	9 Filde Street	
	Rachel	7	"	
Parkinson	Frank	51	Bk Kirkham	
	Frank	17	"	
Pope	Margt	36	5 Cold Bath St	
	Mary	16	"	
	Sally	14	"	
	George	12	"	
	John	9	"	
	Betty	8	"	
	William	5	"	
Park	John	39	Vicar St	
	Jane	42	"	
	James	17	"	
	William	14	"	
	Thomas	13	"	
	Joseph	8	"	
	John	1	"	
Paul	Peter	27	"	
	Catherine	27	"	
	Mary Ann	5	"	
Pert	Ann	63	Walker	
Parkinson	Richard	23	18 "	
Pemberton	James	63	Ribbleton	
	Elizabeth	55	"	
	Mary	17	"	
	Lucy	15	"	
	James	13	"	
	Agnes	10	"	
	Richard	31	"	
Pool	Betty	69	Long Lane	
	Thomas	34	"	
Pike	Thomas		Fulwood	

148

1820 Census — Catholic Congregation of Preston

Surname	Forename(s)	Age	Address	Comm
Parson	William		[Fulwood]	
	Alice		"	
	Mary		"	
	John		"	
Partington	Simon		3 Mounce St	
	Jane			
	Jos	19		
	Robt	17		
	Ralph	14		
Quain	Peter	70	Friargate up Hodgson yard	
	Patrick	30	"	
	Sarah	27	"	
	Jane	3	"	
	Ellen	2	"	
Rawcliff	Sarah	51	2 Spring Gardens	
	George	16	"	
Rawcliff	John	18	8 Cotton Court	
	Ann	13	"	
	Catherine	11	"	
	William	5	"	
Rigby	Ann	60	81 Church	
	Robert	22	"	
	Ann	23	"	
	Mary	20	"	
	Joseph	18	"	
Ratcliff	Mary	19	8 "	
Rishton	Jeffery	80	15 Mince between	
	Margeret	80	"	
Richardson	Margeret	32	25 Fishergate	
Rigg	John	38	Charles St	
	Agnes	38	"	
	Jane	14	"	
	Mary	11	"	
	John	6	"	
	Margeret	3	"	
	James	1	"	
Rishton	Ann	7	32 Mount	
Rigby	James	31	20 "	
	Mary	28	"	
	Isabella	6	"	
Robinson	Richard	33	12 Heatley	
	Betty	30	"	
	Ann	5	"	
	Joseph	4	"	
	Faby	1	"	
Ratcliff	Charles	40	9 Simpson	
	Margeret	42	"	
	Margeret	8	"	
Rigby	Robert	78	19 Ratcliff	
	Richard	50	"	

1820 Census Catholic Congregation of Preston

Surname	Forename(s)	Age	Address	Comm
[Rigby]	James	48	[Ratcliff]	
	Alice	43	"	
	Robert	38	"	
	Elizabeth	22	"	
Robinson	William	16	35 Friargate	
Richardson	John	46	Back Lane	
	Elizabeth	46	"	
	Margeret	18	"	
	Ellen	15	"	
	Alice	11	"	
	Mary Ann	9	"	
	Ann	7	"	
	John	3	"	
Rogerson	Ellen	70	68 "	
Roberts	Mary	42	"	
	Thomas	15	"	
	Robert	11		
Rawcliffe	George		Crows Street	
	Ann		"	
	Alice		"	
Richester	John		"	
	Mary		"	
	James	4	"	
	Joseph	1	"	
Richester	Mickie		"	
	Ann		"	
	Ann	24	"	
Rice	Margt	26	7 Dale	
	Arthur	2	"	
Ray	Barnaby	5	"	
Rion	Bridget	40	21 "	
	James	16	"	
	John	13	"	
Rostrin	Eliza	43	10 Stanley	
Rockliff	Alice	80	5 Canal	
	Mary	36	"	
	Ellen	35	"	
	Ann	15	"	
	Joseph	1	"	
Robinson	John	32	11 "	
	Jane	32	"	
	James	6	"	
	George	2	"	
	Margt	1	"	
Rainforth	Joseph	24	14 "	
	Ann	29	"	
	George	1	"	
Rose	George	28	13 Hope Street	
	Ellen	20	"	
	William	3	"	

1820 Census　　　　Catholic Congregation of Preston

Surname	Forename(s)	Age	Address	Comm
Richardson	Jane	27	15 [Hope Street]	
Riley	A	47	16 "	
Richardson	Jane	27	17 "	
Rainford	Edward	80	Bridge	
	Ann	43	"	
Rawcliff	Robert	20	35 "	
Robinson	Betty	42	24 Bridge St Lane	
	Ann	12	"	
	Jane	9	"	
Rigby	Jane	63	5 Anchor Weind	
Richardson	John	56	105 Friargate	
	Elizabeth	55	"	
	Elizabeth	14	"	
Riley	Thomas	21	108 "	
Rose	James	30	Claytons yard	
	Alice	13	"	
	William	10	"	
	John	8	"	
	Ann	5	"	
Rose	John	33	121 Friargate	
Rigby	William		10 Vauxhall	
	Ann		"	
	Betty	21	"	
	James	20	"	
	Thomas	16	"	
	Ann	14	"	
	William	9	"	
	John	4	"	
	Nicholas	9	"	
Rose	M		"	
	Betsy	15	"	
	Henry	7	"	
Robinson	Richard		Back King	
	Ellen		"	
Riley	Ann		Paradise	
	Margt		"	
	Ellen		"	
	William		"	
Rigby	John		2 Back Grimshaw	
Riley	Jane		25 Bk Queen St	
	Ellen	26	"	
	Peggy	20	"	
	William	15	"	
Rigby	Thomas		3 King	
	Jane		"	
	Mary	5	"	
	John	3	"	
	Ellen	1	"	
Rose	Ann		27 Leeming	
	Alice	17	"	

1820 Census   Catholic Congregation of Preston

Surname	Forename(s)	Age	Address	Comm
[Rose]	Richard	9	[Leeming]	
	Mark	6	"	
	Ann	4	"	
	William	2	"	
Robinson	William		Crows	
	Agnes		"	
	John	4	"	
	Ann	2	"	
	Betty	1	"	
Rock	Peter	33	Shambles	
	Grace	34	"	
	Bella	12	"	
	John	10	"	
	Mary	8	"	
	Maria	6	"	
Rainford	Alice	77	Molyneux Square	
Rigby	Mary	56	M'ket Place	
	Jane	24	"	
Rigby	Ann	32	"	
	Margt	21	"	
Rogerson	Elizabeth	18	"	
Rodder	Henry	6	150 Friargate	
Robinson	Margeret	44	"	
	Ann	18	"	
	William	16	"	
	Elizabeth	13	"	
	John	10	"	
	Margt	1	"	
Richardson	Mary		Turks Head yard	
Roger	Ann		"	
Roskell	Roger		Rose	
	Mary Ann		"	
	Thomas	15	"	
	Robert	13	"	
	James	11	"	
	Nicholas	6	"	
	George	4	"	
	John	1	"	
Rodgett	Thomas	20	96 High	
Rigby	Mary	63	43 "	
	Ellen	23	"	
Rawstron	Mary	40	Fylde	
	Thomas	4	"	
	Henry	2	"	
Robinson	Joseph	37	10 "	
	John	14	"	
	Mary	13	"	
	Nicholas	8	"	
	William	2	"	
Rishton	William	34	6 Snow Hill	

1820 Census   Catholic Congregation of Preston

Surname	Forename(s)	Age	Address	Comm
[Rishton]	Mary	39	[Snow Hill]	
	Magert	13	"	
	Martha	11	"	
	James	10	"	
	Ann	7	"	
	Richard	2	"	
Rishton	John	74	36 Snow Hill	53
	Mary	61	"	
Rely	John	39	Vicars	
Richardson	Thomas	48	Water lane end	
	Mary	17	"	
	Thomas	15	"	
	Ralph	14	"	
	Evan	13	"	
	Margt	11	"	
	Ann	9	"	
	Alice	6	"	
	Martha	5	"	
Rigby	William		Fulwood	
	James		"	
	Henry		"	
	George		"	
	Peggy		"	
	Ann		"	
Robinson	Edward		"	
	Thomas		"	
Rigby	Richard		"	
	Alice		"	
	Mary		"	
Rigby	Robert		"	
	Ellen		"	
	Ann		"	
	Ellen		"	
	James		"	
	John		"	
	Thomas		"	
Shakeshaff	Henry	60	29 Church Street	
	Mary	57	"	
	Grace	70	"	
	Betty	34	"	
Stanley	Henry	29	"	
	Betty	28	"	
Swindlehurst	Lucy	40	9 Spring Gardens	
	Ellen	18	"	
	Thomas	16	"	
	Ann	13	"	
	Elizabeth	4	"	
	Christopher	2	9 Spring Gardens	
Smith	John	38	16 Nile	
	Alice	36	"	

1820 Census — Catholic Congregation of Preston

Surname	Forename(s)	Age	Address	Comm
[Smith]	Grace	17	[Nile]	
	Richard	15	"	
	Betsy	13	"	
	Silvester	11	"	
	Alice	7	"	
	Mary	4	"	
	Ellen	2	"	
	Motilda	1	"	
Southworth	Ellen	22	119 Church	
Strange	Margeret	23	6 Holden yard	
	William	4	"	
	Thomas	2	"	
	James	1	"	
Sherrington	Henry	24	105 Church	
	Lucy	24	"	
Stizzaker	Nancy	39	5 "	
	William	14	"	
	Mary Ann	12	"	
	Eliza	10	"	
	Margeret	8	"	
Siddell	John	40	21 Mince between	
	Sicily	40	"	
	Frederick	16	"	
	Thomas	13	"	
	Rd	12	"	
	John	10	"	
	Mary Ann	8	"	
	Elizabeth	6	"	
	Ellen	4	"	
Sumner	Thomas	45	Evenham	
	Jane	39	"	
	Betsy	18	"	
	Rosa	15	"	
	James	14	"	
	Richard	3	"	
	Margeret	1	"	
Shape	Thomas	48	147 Church	
Sharrock	Winefrid	58	8 Woodcocks yard	
	Mary	59	"	
Sacil	William	24	29 Fishergate	
	John	7	"	
	Margeret	4	"	
	Richard	1	"	
Seed	Robert	36	30 Fishergate	
	Dorothy	34	"	
	Richard	9	"	
	Ann	7	"	
	Alice	4	"	
	Robert	1	"	
Simmons	Robert	20	31 "	

1820 Census   Catholic Congregation of Preston

Surname	Forename(s)	Age	Address	Comm
Shaw	Joseph	23	[Fishergate]	
Sidgreaves	George	35	"	
Swarbrick	Mary	13	42 "	
Sherrington	Henry		1 West end	
	Ellen		"	
	William		"	
	John		"	
Seed	John	44	St Wilfrid	
	Ann	33	"	
	John	11	"	
	Mary Ann	9	"	
	Elizabeth	7	"	
	Richard	3	"	
	Robert	1	"	
Sager	Margeret		Winkley Place	
Smith	Henry	46	9 Cannon	
	Mary	39	"	
	Jane	17	"	
	James	15	"	
	Henry	13	"	
	George	10	"	
	Richard	7	"	
	Thomas	5	"	
	Maria	2	"	
Scott	Elizabeth	30?	12 "	44
Scannell	John	50?	27 Mount	44
	Elizabeth	35	"	
	John	13	"	
	Ann	10	"	
Sudell	William	35	19 "	
	Mary Ann	19	"	
	Jane	14	"	
Smith	Sarah	38	17 "	
	Maria	19	"	
Shepherd	William	58	Town Hall	
	Peggy	54	"	
	Margeret	19	"	
	John	15	"	
	Ann	4	"	
	Thomas	2	"	
Smith	Eliza	13	10 Mount Pleasant	
Singleton	Ellen	34	4 Heatley	
Smith	John	33	7 Talbot	
	Nancy	3	"	
	Margeret	1	"	
Stepenson	John	47	33 Friargate	
	Mary	51	"	
	Jane	20	"	
	Elizabeth	10	"	
Stephenson	William	27	36 Friargate	

1820 Census   Catholic Congregation of Preston

Surname	Forename(s)	Age	Address	Comm
[Stephenson]	Elizabeth	34	[Friargate]	
	John	10	"	
	Lawrence	3	"	
	James	1	"	
Sharrock	Mary		35 "	
	Grace		"	
Swarbrick	John	22	3 Hill	
Southworth	Hugh	35	4 "	
	Margeret	34	"	
	John	10	"	
	Alice	8	"	
	Margeret	5	"	
	Mary Ann	2	"	
Sagar	Adam	58	Friargate	
	Ann	58	"	
	William	18	"	
Seed	Teressa	33	Lills yard	
	Thomas	6	"	
	Robert	4	"	
	John	1	"	
Starkie	William	43	Union	
	Ellen	33	"	
Smithies	Thomas	71	Friargate	
	Elizabeth	71	"	
	Elizabeth	36	"	
	Mary	32	"	
Smith	Christr	29	"	
	Mary	33	"	
	James	9	"	
	Margt	7	"	
	Ann	2	"	
Saul	Mary	56	64 "	
	Thomas	16	"	
	Elizabeth	14	"	
Simmons	Sally	70	100 "	
Sherlikar	John	15	Prescotts yard	
Sherrington	Jane	18	107 Friargate	
Sharples	Ann	29	108 "	
	Elizabeth	8	"	
	Jane	6	"	
	Ann	1	"	
Smith	Jane	16	"	
Sidgreaves	John	78	127 "	
Stains	John		13 Vauxhall	
	Betty		"	
	William	17	"	
	Richard	10	"	
	Maria	4	"	
	Eliza	2	"	
Sharples	Catherine		10 "	

1820 Census   Catholic Congregation of Preston

Surname	Forename(s)	Age	Address	Comm
Sharples	Catherine		10 Vauxhall	
Slater	Margt	20	"	
Slater	Ann		Park St	
	Bella		"	
Sharrock	John	9	9 Charlotte	
	Ellen		"	
Sagar	Bridget		Bk King	
Shepherd	Debbra		"	
Slater	James		"	
	Elizabeth		"	
Scott	Mrs		Walton	
Still	Mary		William	
Smith	John		Paradise	
Slater	Charles		16 Leeming	
Swarbrick	Alice		2 Queen	
Sanderson	Margeret	50	"	
Singleton	John	20	"	
	Betty		"	
	Jane		"	
Slater	John		12 Duke	
	Bella		"	
	William	13	"	
	Mary	10	"	
	Bella	7	"	
	Betty	3	"	
	John	1	"	
Smith	James		Top of Duke	
	Alice		"	
Snape	Mary		"	
Smith	Nicholas	6	"	
	Mary	3	"	
	Ann	1	"	
Siberin	Ellen		"	
Sandham	Thomas		8 King	
	Alice		"	
	Ellen	9		
	Ann	9		
	Alice	3	"	
	Jane	1	"	
Shepherd	William		17 "	
	Mary		"	
	Elizabeth	2	"	
Slater	Ann		9 Park	
	Bella		"	
Smith	Alice		Craggs Street	
	Thomas	9	"	
Smith	William		Moore lane	
	Margt		"	
	Mary	9	"	
	John	6	"	

157

1820 Census Catholic Congregation of Preston

Surname	Forename(s)	Age	Address	Comm
[Smith]	Ann	3	[Moore lane]	
	Margt	1	"	
Swarbrick	Adam		"	
	Margeret		"	
Smith	John		Crows	
	Richard	2	"	
	Mary	1	"	
Stephenson	Ann		"	
	James	12	"	
	Absolum	10	"	
	Rachel	3	"	
	William	1	"	
Simpson	Joseph		"	
	Betty		"	
Shorrock	William		"	
	Ann		"	
	Margeret	8	"	
	James	6	"	
	Mary	1	"	
Smith	Thomas	45	9 Ribbleton Lane	
	Margt	35	"	
	Ellen	3	"	
	Vincent	1	"	
Smith	James	40	12 "	
	Mary	40	"	
	Jane	18	"	
	Thomas	17	"	
	Richard	13	"	
	Nancy	10	"	
	John	8	"	
	Elizabeth	6	"	
	William	2	"	
Shakshaft	John	70	13 "	
	Sarah	63		
	William	32	"	
Shakshaft	Edward	36	14 "	
	Agnes	32	"	
	John	1	"	
Sumner	Rosy	50	1 "	
Salsburry	Eliza	38	10 Dail St	
	Nancy	18	"	
	John	15	"	
	Henry	6	"	
Sherrington	James	42	12 Dale St	
	Emery	45	"	
	John	20	"	
	Mary	11	"	
Sheel	Hugh	60	13 Stanley	
Southworth	James	52	8 Frederick	
	William	22	"	

1820 Census — Catholic Congregation of Preston

Surname	Forename(s)	Age	Address	Comm
[Southworth]	Eliza	17	[Frederick]	
	Agnes	15	"	
	Charlotte	12	"	
	Stephen	7	"	
Smith	Thomas	43	6 Richmond Row	
	Sarah	40	"	
	George	18	"	
	Robert	16	"	
	James	10	"	
	Mary	8	"	
	Agnes	4	"	
	William		"	
	Nancy	2	"	
Sumner	Robert	60	Bk of House of Correction	
	Mary	61	"	
	Robert	22	"	
Simson	Christr	62	4 Moorside	
	Mary	56	"	
Smith	Richard	45	Canal	
	Nancy	37	"	
	Thomas	15	"	
	Mary	13	"	
	Jane	12	"	
	Alice	10	"	
	Susan	9	"	
	Richard	5	"	
Sherlikar	Thomas	40	12 "	
	Ellen	39	"	
	Joseph	18	"	
	John	16	"	
	Thomas	15	"	
	Robert	11	"	
	Edward	8	"	
	Henry	3	"	
	Ellen	1	"	
Sharrock	Ralph	66	15 Hope St	
	Jane	56	"	
Singleton	William	29	27 Canal	
	Lucy	29	"	
	Thomas	9	"	
	John	6	"	
	Ellen	4	"	
	Henry	3	"	
Simson	Richard	34	Ansons Square	
	Margt	34	"	
	Bella	14	"	
	Richard	12	"	
	Mary	8	"	
	Ann	5	"	
	Margt	3	"	

1820 Census   Catholic Congregation of Preston

Surname	Forename(s)	Age	Address	Comm
Sharrock	Catherine	64	Fosters Square	
	Catherine	17	"	
Slater	Thomas	38	"	
	Betty	32	"	
	Margeret	6	"	
	John	3	"	
Singleton	Joseph	27	Bk Canal	
	Kitty	28	"	
	Thomas	6	"	
	Margeret	4	"	
Smith	James	60	2 Bridge	
	Margt	60	"	
	Ann	20	"	
	Margt	17	"	
	James	14	"	
	Margt	9	"	
Simpson	Betty	20	5 Sopery	
	Mary	2	"	
	Easter	1	"	
Simpson	William	41	10 "	
	Betty	36	"	
	William	14	"	
	John	8	"	
	Nancy	5	"	
	Richard	2	"	
	Catherine	2	"	
Snape	Robert		Field Road	
	Catherine		"	
Smith	Bella	10	"	
Smith	Betty		Friday St	
Swarbrick	Betty		"	
Siddell	Ellen		"	
Smith	Henry	33	Back Lane	
	Mary	28	"	
	Margeret	1	"	
Shakshaft	Thomas	45	5 Back Horse Yard	
	Mary	39	"	
	Henry	15	"	
	Robert	14	"	
	Thomas	12	"	
	John	11	"	
	Mary	10	"	
	Joseph	3	"	
Spencer	Daniel	23	12 Hardmans Yard	
	Sarah	26	"	
	John	1	"	
Spencer	John	54	6 Mellings Yard	
	Margt	49	"	
	John	13	"	
	Bridget	11	"	

1820 Census — Catholic Congregation of Preston

Surname	Forename(s)	Age	Address	Comm
[Spencer]	Jane	8	[Mellings Yard]	
Shakshaft	Law	52	16 Shambles	
	Ann	19	"	
	Sarah	18	"	
	Ellen	9	"	
	Hannah	6	"	
Shepherd	Jane	30	15 "	
Shepherd	Richard	50	Gin Bow entry	
	Mary	46	"	
Smith	Emma	27	Market Place	
Savage	Ann		Waterworths Yard	
Stockley	Margt	49	29 Friargate	
	Mary	20	"	
	John	19	"	
Swarbrick	John	36	1 Slaters Yard	
	Betsy	35	"	
	George	12	"	
	Thomas	10	"	
	James	8	"	
	William	7	"	
Saul	John		Friargate	
	Alice	22	"	
	Mary	1	"	
Salsbury	Ellen	35	" Gas Shop Yard	
Singleton	John	54	14 Friargate	
	Ann	55	"	
	John	27	"	
	William	18	"	
	Richard	14	"	
	Ellen	3	"	
Swarbrick	Thomas		30 Pleasant	
	Joseph		"	
Sudle	Richard		Sike Hill	
	Nancy		"	
	Henry	10	"	
	Richard	8	"	
	Ellen	6	"	
	Mary	3	"	
	Joseph	3	"	
Shakshaft	Law		Stonygate	
	Mary		"	
	Richard	18	"	
	Alice	17	"	
	John	11	"	
	Betsy	6	"	
Swarbrick	George		5 Rose	
	Margeret		"	
	Jane	7	"	
	Thomas	5	"	
	Mary	1	"	

1820 Census   Catholic Congregation of Preston

Surname	Forename(s)	Age	Address		Comm
Stamming	Ellen		10	[Rose]	
	Ellen	3		"	
Smith	Thomas	62	92	High Street	
	Margeret	60		"	
	Ann	22		"	
	James	8		"	
Smith	John	23	7	"	
	Helen	23		"	
	Ann	4		"	
	Mary	1		"	
Simpson	Michal			Everton Gardens	
	Mrs			"	
	Bridget	10		"	
	Ann	9		"	
	Sarah	6		"	
	Joseph	3		"	
	Mary Ann	2		"	
Stubs	Ellen	25		8 Whitakers row	
Sudle	George	50	12	"	
	Mary	23		"	
	John	14		"	
	Nancy	16		"	
	Joseph	12		"	
	Jane	5		"	
	Thomas	2		"	
Sherrington	Jane	60x		Emmets Shop	
	Edward	60x		"	54
	Edward	22x		"	
	William	15x		"	
Smith	William	58		Filde Street	
	Ann	21		"	
	Sally	19		"	
	Mary	16		"	
	William	14		"	
	Ann	12		"	
	Easter	9		"	
	Thomas	5		"	
Smith	John	59	17	"	
	Ann	51		"	
	Thomas	28		"	
	William	26		"	
	Robert	24		"	
	John	22		"	
	Mary	20		"	
	Alice	16		"	
	Rachel	13		"	
	Joseph	10		"	
Sumner	Joseph	27	10	"	
	Maria	3		"	
	Mary	1		"	

1820 Census   Catholic Congregation of Preston

Surname	Forename(s)	Age	Address	Comm
Simpson	Thomas	33	15 Cold Bath St	
	Ann	39	"	
	Betty	11	"	
	Thomas	8	"	
	John	6	"	
	Henry	4	"	
	Alice	2	"	
	Jane	1	"	
Spencer	James	26	1 Bolton St	
	Mary	23	"	
	Jane	1	"	
Shannon	Martin	56	15 Bolton St	
	Betty	45	"	
Shepherd	Thomas	39	17 Snow hill	
	Margt	45	"	
	Robert	16	"	
	Richard	15	"	
	James	13	"	
	Mary	11	"	
	Joseph	7	"	
	Thomas	5	"	
	Betty	2	"	
Seed	Richard	35	18 "	
	Elizabeth	32	"	
	William	4	"	
	Ann	2	"	
Savage	Jane	25	23 "	
	John	3	"	
	Jane	1	"	
Salsbury	Francis	21	2 Vicar	
Spencer	Margt	32	"	
Smith	Mary	27	31 "	
Standing	Jane	9	"	55
	Peter	7	"	
Siddons	Benjamin	63	Ribbleton	
	Jane	62	"	
	Alice	33	"	
	Peter	31	"	
Stock	Edward	50	Tulketh Hall	
	Mary	50		
	Michael	18		
	Edward	16		
	Catherine	15		
	John	14		
Singleton	Thomas	27	Ashton Brows	
	Ellin	31	"	
	Alice	6	"	
	Betty	4	"	
	John	1	"	
Smith	William		Fulwood	

1820 Census   Catholic Congregation of Preston

Surname	Forename(s)	Age	Address	Comm
[Smith]	Alice		[Fulwood]	
	Margt		"	
Smith	William		Fulwood	
	Betty		"	
	John		"	
Slater	John		"	
	Ann		"	
	John		"	
Singleton	John		5 Richmond Row	
	Margrt		"	
	Ann	2	"	
	Martha	1	"	
Tipping	Thomas	55	34 Church St	
	Jane	48	"	
	William	20	"	
	Ann	18	"	
	Hannah	16	"	
	Mary	14	"	
	Thomas	11	"	
	Margeret	8	"	
	Catherine Agnes	3	"	
Thompson	John	21	10 Cockyard	
	Mary	14	"	
Tomlinson	John	47	25 Fishergate	
	Margeret	47	"	
	Ellen	18	"	
	Eliza	15	"	
	Emma	13	"	
Tomlins	Sarah	24	35 "	
Talbot	William		40 "	
	Catherine		"	
	Dorothy	19	"	
	Elizabeth	15	"	
	Margeret		"	
	Mary Ann		"	
Turner	John	21	45 "	
Tabernor	Isabella	20	Theatre St	
Turner	George	60	"	
	Elizabeth	60	"	
	John	25	"	
	Ann	27	"	
Teebay	Lawrence		57 Fishergate	
	Mary	46	"	
	Richard		"	
	Anthony	40	71 "	
	Mary	27	"	
	Jane	5	"	
	James	4	"	
	Richard	3	"	
	Mary	1	"	

1820 Census   Catholic Congregation of Preston

Surname	Forename(s)	Age	Address	Comm
Taylor	Elizabeth	16	7 St Wilfrid	
Turner	John	30	2 Fox St	
	Alice	32	"	
	Robert	4	"	
	Mary Ann	1	"	
Tearney	Alice	14	12 Cannon	
Taylor	Ruth	75	16 Chapel	
Talbot	Alice	56	10 "	
Taylor	Margeret	44	6 Mount Pleasant	
	Ellen	21	"	
	John	20	"	
	Jane	16	"	
	Ann	9	"	
	Betsy	6	"	
Taylor	Ellen	19	61 Friargate	
Turner	Thomas	53	21 Heatley St	
	Mary	48	"	
	Jane	22	"	
	John	20	"	
	Mary	14	"	
	Joseph	12	"	
	George	10	"	
	Margeret	9	"	
	Thomas	7	"	
Tootle	Winifrid	60	4 "	
Thompson	James	30	10 Talbot	
	Betsy	33	"	
	Thomas	8	"	
	Ann	4	"	
Tenant	Margeret	25	"	
	Mary	7	"	
	Ann	1	"	
Tomlinson	Prissilla	37	Friargate	
	Elizabeth	15	"	
	Mary	13	"	
	George	9	"	
	John	1	"	
Turner	William	37	Back Lane	
	Isabella	38	"	
	John	15	"	
	James	12	"	
	Ellen	8	"	
	Elizabeth	5	"	
	William	4	"	
	Martin	1	"	
Townson	John	22	"	
Townsend	James	55	50 Friargate	
	Jane	43	"	
	James	20	"	
	Richard	16	"	

1820 Census   Catholic Congregation of Preston

Surname	Forename(s)	Age	Address	Comm
[Townsend]	Mary	14	[Friargate]	
	Margt	12	"	
	Andrew	9	"	
	William	7	"	
	Elizabeth	1	"	
Taylor	John	55	68 "	
	Mary	50	"	
	Elizabeth	24	"	
	Jane	19	"	
	John	17	"	
	Joseph	15	"	
	Ellen	12	"	
	Thomas	8	"	
	Ann	6	"	
Taylor	John	40	107 Friargate	
	Ann	35	"	
	Margt	13	"	
	Mary	11	"	
	James	8	"	
	Ann	6	"	
	William	5	"	
	Elizabeth	1	"	
Taylor	Ann	53	121 "	
Tengh	Betty		3 Vauxhall Road	
Towers	Thomas		10 Charlotte	
	Ann		"	
	Robert	13	"	
	John	12	"	
	Jane	11	"	
	Edward	10	"	
	Peggy	9	"	
	Thomas	8	"	
	Nancy	7	"	
	Mary	6	"	
	Alice	5	"	
	Elizabeth	2	"	
	Bridget	1	"	
Taylor	Betty		Paradise	
Thompson	James		10 Leeming	
	Alice		"	
	Mary		"	
Tootal	Ann		Top of Duke	
Twist	John		20 King	
	Ann		"	
	James		"	
	George		"	
Talbot	Margt		Paradise	
Taylor	Ann		Craggs	
	John	3	"	
	Mary	1	"	

1820 Census — Catholic Congregation of Preston

Surname	Forename(s)	Age	Address	Comm
Traysay	Sarah		Moore lane	
	Mary Ann	8	"	
Tulley	Mary		"	
Talbot	Roger	66	1 Thomas	
	Ellen	36	"	
	Kiddy	20	"	
Taylor	John	40	7 Bread	
	Ann	43	"	
Thornton	Ellen	52	31 Bridge	
	Margt	19	"	
	John	18	"	
	James	13	"	
Townley	Richard	62	39 Bridge Street	
	Betty	18	"	
Townley	Margeret	62	11 Bridge Street Lane	
	Robert	24	"	
	Richard	22	"	
	Charles	18	"	
Townley	Thomas	28	"	
	Mary	25	"	
	John	5	"	
	Robert	4	"	
	Ellen	1	"	
Townley	Mary	40	15 Spring	
	Nancy	4	"	
Taylor	James	70	73 Back Lane	
	Betty	75	"	
	Peter	37	"	
Thornton	Ellen	45	Molyneux Square	
	John	22	"	
	Robert	19	"	
	James	9	"	
Townsend	Charles	25	18 Shambles	
Taylor	James	19	"	
Taylor	Mary	15	Market Place	
Turner	James	30	Lune St	
Thompson	Jane		Bostock St	
	Mary Ann	11	"	
Threnan	Richard		22 High St	
Taylor	James	47	Vicar Street	
	Thomas	12	"	
Tootle	John	58	11 "	
	Isabella	59	"	
Taylor	Jane	27	Marshend	
	William	3	"	
Thompson	Henry	36	Ashton Brows	
	Ellen	28	"	
	Jane	8	"	
	James	6	"	
	John	4	"	

1820 Census   Catholic Congregation of Preston

Surname	Forename(s)	Age	Address	Comm
[Thompson]	William	2	[Ashton Brows]	
Taylor	Mary		Fulwood	
	Robert		"	
	Joseph		"	
	Mary		"	
	Ellen		"	
	John		"	
Taylor	Thomas		"	
	Mary		"	
	Betty		"	
Unsworth	Thomas		18 Mount St	
	Ann	15	"	
	Jane	13	"	
	Mary	12	"	
	Thomas	10	"	
	Elizabeth	8	"	
	James	7	"	
	Helen	5	"	
Uedle	William	14	10 Vauxhall	
	Ann	10	"	
	John	13	"	
Urgney	Henry	60	Canal	
Unsworth	Bella	52	Water Lane end	
	Betty	18	"	
	Richard	13	"	
	John	11	"	
	Margt	6	"	
Valentine	Elizabeth	32	46 Fishergate	
Valentine	Alice	77	22 Mount	
Vose	John	40	40 Stanley	
	Ann	36	"	
Valentine	Margt	12	23 High	
	Richard	10	"	
Woodacre	William	67	15 St John Street	
	Jane	64	"	
Worden	Joseph	27	62 Church Street	
	Peter	32	"	
Wilcock	John	31	18 Spring Gardens	
	Julia	30	"	
	Ann	7 ·	"	
Walker	Thomas	44	"	
Walton	Mary	70	"	
Whiteside	Joseph	15	23 Church	
Wagstaff	Sarah	23	8 "	
Walker	John	24	32 Mince between	
Winder	Mary	48	8 "	
	John	22	"	
	James	20	"	
	Ann	18	"	
	Peggy	16	"	

1820 Census — Catholic Congregation of Preston

Surname	Forename(s)	Age	Address	Comm
[Winder]	Mary	14	[Mince between]	
	Catherine	9	"	
	Jenny	7	"	
	Ellen	3	"	
Wilcock	Betty	18	115 Church	
Whitehead	James	23	8 Fishergate	
Woodcock	Alice		3 Woodcocks yard	
	Mary		"	
Wilcock	James	42	26 Fishergate	
	Mary	43	"	
	John	15	"	
	Jane	13	"	
	Margeret	11	"	
	Frank	10	"	
	Mary	8	"	
	Catherine	3	"	
	Ann	1	"	
Wilson	George	45	31 "	
	Ellen	29	"	
	Mary	6	"	
	John	2	"	
	Henry	1	"	
Walton	Isabella	70	2 Butlers Court	
	Oliver	28	3 "	
	Ellen	23	"	
	Maria	4		
	Ellen	2	"	
	Elizabeth	1	"	
Ward	Margeret	42	40 Fishergate	
William	Ellen	20	"	
Walker	Ann		1 West end	
Whitehead	Elizabeth	32	Fishergate	
Wollick	Mary Alice		16 Cannon	
Woodcock	Mary	48	38 Mount	
	Jane	17	"	
Westhead	George	27	33 "	
	Mary	31	"	
	Ann	3	"	
	Alice	1		
Walker	John	22	15 Mount St	
Whittam	Jane	58	12 "	
	Joseph	20	"	
Westhead	Ann	58	10 Chapel	
Walker	William	25	3 New Cock yard	
Woodhouse	Betsy	48	6 Mount Pleasant	
	William	21	"	
	Thomas	17	"	
	Richard	12	"	
	Robert	6	"	
Wareing	Mary	43	24 Heatley	

1820 Census   Catholic Congregation of Preston

Surname	Forename(s)	Age	Address	Comm
Winstanley	Helen	45	5 Ratcliff	
	Hannah	11	"	
	Elizabeth	9	"	
Walker	Ellen	58	14 "	
Wilkinson	Jane	60	"	
Whittle	Peter	53	6 Hill	
	Mary	58	"	
	Matthew	29	"	
Wareing	John	12	"	
Westray	Thomas	25	1 Snow Hill	
	Mary	23	"	
	James	2	"	
	Jane	2	"	
Wiggans	Thomas	63	Lills Yard	
	Ellen	63	"	
	James	27	"	
Welsh	Robert	43	Back Lane	
	Ann	43	"	
	Margery	18	"	
	Jane	13	"	
	George	12	"	
	John	9	"	
	Margt	7	"	
	Ruth	5	"	
Woods	Peter	52	52 Friargate	
	Martha	54	"	
	Martha	14	"	
Wilcock	Margt	20	"	
Wignal	Ann	66	65 "	
	Grace	21	"	
Wilding	Robert	44	101 "	
	Ann	44	"	
	Maria	3	"	
Wiggins	Thomas	80	"	
Waring	Elizabeth	42	7 Prescotts yard	
	Ellen	21	"	
	James	6	"	
Wareing	Thomas	58	128 Friargate	
	Elizabeth	58	"	
	Ann	22	"	
	Mary	19	"	
	Ruth	17	"	
	Elizabeth	15	"	
Wareing	John	26	"	
	Joseph	26	"	
	Ellen	26	"	
	Thomas	5	"	
	Elizabeth	2	"	
	Ellen	1	"	
Woodcock	Thomas		28 Vauxhall	

1820 Census — Catholic Congregation of Preston

Surname	Forename(s)	Age	Address	Comm
[Woodcock]	Nancy		[Vauxhall]	
	Francis	17	"	
	Betty	15	"	
	Margeret	11	"	
	George	10	"	
	John	8	"	
	James	5	"	
	Thomas	4	"	
	Henry	2	"	
	Mary	1	"	
Worsley	Roger		10 "	
	Mary		"	
Walmsley	James		8 Bk Charlotte	
	Thomas	4	"	
	Mary	3	"	
	William	1	"	
Walmsley	Jane		5 Charlotte	
	Ellen		"	
	Thos		"	
	Ann	17	"	
Wareing	George		"	
	Margeret		"	
	George	16	"	
Ward	Mary		Bk King	
	Ann	12	"	
	Mary	8	"	
	Alice	4	"	
	Henry	2	"	
Whittle	George		"	
	Mary		"	
Wilding	Alice		"	
	Catherine	14	"	
	Ellen	8	"	
	Ann	5	"	
Whiteside	Miss		Walton	
Wilcock	John		William	
	John	16	"	
Wilson	John		Leeming	
	Betty	12	"	
	Jane	10	"	
Winstanley	William		30 Duke	
	Ellen		"	
	Ann		"	
	William	15	"	
	Peter	12	"	
	Joseph	12	"	
Whiteside	George		11 King	
	Catherine	19	"	
	George	12	"	
	Bella	7	"	

1820 Census   Catholic Congregation of Preston

Surname	Forename(s)	Age	Address	Comm
[Whiteside]	John	6		
	Margt	5	"	
	Agnes	2	"	
Woods	Ellen	13	"	
Worthington	Thomas	25	"	
	Jane		"	
	John	28	"	
	James	24	"	
	Mathew	18	"	
	Jane	20	"	
	Thomas	13	"	
	Mary	8	"	
Woodruff	Henry	27	"	
	Margt		"	
	James	14	"	
	Mary	10	"	
	Ellen	9	"	
Watson	Henry		Paradise	
	Ann		"	
Whittle	Peggy		"	
Worthington	Richard	32	"	
Woodcock	John		Singleton Row	
	Betty		"	
	Isabella	17	"	
	Ann	13	"	
	Thomas	10	"	
	John	7	"	
	Rachel	5	"	
	Mary	2	"	
	Elizabeth	1	"	
Walker	John	50	"	
	Ann		"	
Wearden	Dorothy	39	Singleton Row	
	Margt	26	"	
	Betty	8	"	
	Ellen	4	"	
	James	3	"	
Waterhouse	Richard	26	"	
	Mary		"	
	Betty		"	
Worden	Alice	20	"	
	Ellen	16	"	
	Jane	10	"	
	James	8	"	
Whalley	Robert	19	"	
	Ann		"	
	Joseph	10	"	
	Mary	7	"	
Woodcock	George	16	"	
	Ellen		"	

1820 Census   Catholic Congregation of Preston

Surname	Forename(s)	Age	Address	Comm
[Woodcock]	Mary Ann	13	[Singleton Row]	
	Jane	11	"	
	Ann	6	"	
	Elizabeth	2	"	
Waterhouse	Martin	10	"	
	Ellen		"	
	Alice	8	"	
	Ann	5	"	
	Elizabeth	3	"	
Woodroff	Charles		4 Singleton's Row	
	Ann		"	
Waterhouse	Margt		Craggs row	
	Thomas	16	"	
	William		"	
	Mary		"	
	Agnes	14	"	
	William	12	"	
Whittle	James		Moore lane	
	Jane		"	
	Sarah	20	"	
	Betty	17	"	
	Henry	15	"	
	Jane	13	"	
	Margt	8	"	
Waterhouse	James		"	
	Betty		"	
	Mary	11	"	
	Jane	9	"	
	Thomas	8	"	
	Alice	6	"	
	James	4	"	
	Betty	2	"	
	Alice		"	
	Betty		"	
Woodroff	John		Moore lane	
	Alice		"	
	Ann	3	"	
	William	1	"	
Walmsley	Mary		Harrison hill	
	Margt	12	"	
	Jane	9	"	
	James	7	"	
	Joseph	4	"	
	Thomas	1	"	
Whalley	William		"	
	Betty		"	
	John	11	"	
	Agnes	6	"	
	Isabella	1	"	
Wearden	Edward		Crows	

1820 Census   Catholic Congregation of Preston

Surname	Forename(s)	Age	Address	Comm
[Wearden]	Ann		[Crows]	
	Ann	5	"	
	Margt	4	"	
	Mary	1	"	
Wilcock	James		"	
	Margeret		"	
	Ellen	9	"	
	Thomas	8	"	
	Robert	5	"	
Wilding	Joseph		"	
	Betty		"	
	George	15	"	
	Thomas	13	"	
	John	7	"	
	Joseph	5	"	
	Jane	3	"	
Waring	John	60	6 Ribbleton lane	
	Elizabeth	59	"	
	James	26	"	
	Thomas	20	"	
	Henry	16	"	
Walmsley	James	60	7 Dale	
	Agnes	60	"	
Willacy	James	36	6 "	
	Mary	37	"	
	James	15	"	
	Margt	13	"	
Walmsley	William	75	20 Dale	
	Nancy	67	"	
Waring	William	18	31 Stanley	
Walmsley	Thomas	15	"	
Waring	John	56	37 "	
	Mary	60	"	
Woens	Robert	42	3 John	
	Ann	48	"	
	Alice	18	"	
	John	11	"	
Whittle	John	60	9 Ann	
	Margt	62	"	
	Ann	35	"	
	Margeret	31	"	
	Thomas	29	"	
	John	26	"	
	Eliza	20	"	
Waring	Thomas	40	9 Frederick	
	Ann	42	"	
	John	17	"	
	Joseph	14	"	
	William	12	"	
	Thomas	10	"	

1820 Census — Catholic Congregation of Preston

Surname	Forename(s)	Age	Address	Comm
[Waring]	Mary	5	[Frederick]	
	Jane	1	"	
Waterhouse	Richard	46	7 Richmond row	
	Jane	44	"	
	James	21	"	
	Eliza	18	"	
	William	16	"	
	Ellen	11	"	
	Thomas	10	"	
Waring	John	29	3 Moorside	
	Eliza	28	"	
	James	4	"	
	Thomas	2	"	
Wake	William	37	Canal	
	Easter	38	"	
	Ann	12	"	
	William	7	"	
	Elizabeth	5	"	
	John	4	"	
	Alice	1	"	
Walmsley	Richard	36	Canal Street	
	Margeret	35	"	
	Jane	11	"	
	Charles	7	"	
	Ann	5	"	
	William	2	"	
Watson	Lucy	31	"	
	John	12	"	
	Margt	10	"	
	Joseph	7	"	
	Ellen	5	"	
Willon	Elizabeth	54	14 Hope Street	
Wilson	Thomas	16	15 "	
Wilcock	Richard	54	Ansons Square	
	Alice	53	"	
	Robert	32	"	
	John	17	"	
	Gregory	12	"	
West	Nancy	27	Fosters Square	
Wilson	Thomas	28	6 Hope Street	
	Jane	28	"	
	Jane		"	
Wadcher	Edward	80	28 Bridge	
Walmsley	James	60	8 "	
	Ellen	48	"	
	John	37	"	
	James	28	"	
	William	22	"	
	Mary	20	"	
	Ann	17	"	

1820 Census　　　　Catholic Congregation of Preston

Surname	Forename(s)	Age	Address	Comm
[Walmsley]	Ellen	15	[Bridge]	
Wareing	Joseph	33	Bridge St Lane	
	Ann	25	"	
	John	3	"	
Wilkinson	Henry	31	14 Canal	
	William	6	"	
	John	2	"	
Worswick	Jane	21	Friday Street	
Wallice	Alice		"	
	John	13	"	
	Thomas	10	"	
	Ann	5	"	
	James	3	"	
Winsley	Roger		Friday Street	
	Mary	1	"	
Wilcock	James		"	
	Ellen		"	
	Richard	8	"	
	Mary	6	"	
	Mary Teresa	6	"	
Worden	George	74	71 Bk Lane	
	Alice	51	"	
	William	13	"	
	Emma	10	"	
Wilkinson	James	35	5 Friargate	
	Sarah	35	"	
	Mary	9	"	
Whittam	William	25	6 "	
	Margeret	25	"	
	Jane	3	"	
	Mary	2	"	
	John	1	"	
Whittle	Peter	30	7 "	
	Nancy	18	"	
	Henry	16	"	
Wilson	Thomas	8	16 "	
Wilkinson	I H	41	11 "	
	Ellen	35	"	
Wallis	Mary	55	11 Hardmans Yard	
Willacy	Thomas	25	5 Mellings Yard	
	Betty	39	"	
Watson	John	68	Shambles	
	Margt	28	"	
	Ann	26	"	
Worden	James	12	Gin Bow entry	
Worthington	Wm	26	"	
Walmsley	Ann	22	5 "	
Worden	Thomas	16	3 Market Place	
Winstanley	Edward	34	150 Friargate	
	Rosa	33	"	

1820 Census   Catholic Congregation of Preston

Surname	Forename(s)	Age	Address	Comm
[Winstanley]	Henry	6	[Friargate]	
	Edward	5	"	
	Rosa	4	"	
	Charles	2	"	
Wilding	Ellen		Friargate Browns Yard	
Woods	James	43	Friargate	
	Betty	44	"	
	John	24	"	
	James	20	"	
Wike	Thomas	40	165 "	
	Margeret	40	"	
	Richard	11	"	
Walker	Thomas		49 Pleasant	
	Mary		"	
	John	9	"	
	Isabella	3	"	
	Edward	5	"	
Worden	Robert		47 "	
	Ann		"	
	William	21	"	
	Mary	20	"	
	John	17	"	
	Joseph	14	"	
	Michael	10	"	
	Jane	7	"	
	Thomas	5	"	
	James	4	"	
Whiteside	Robert		Turks Head Yard	
	Alice		"	
	Mary	4	"	
	William	2	"	
Welsh	James	58	47 High	
	Mary	63	"	
Waterworth	John	45	58 "	
	Agnes	34	"	
	Agnes	9	"	
	John	7	"	
	Richard	5	"	
	Frank	2	"	
Whittle	Robert	64	103 "	
	Margeret	28	"	
	Ann	26	"	
Whiteside	Easter	31	96 "	
Woolf	Thomas	23	109 "	
	Betty	21	"	
Welsh	Joseph	33	79 High St	
	Margt	29	"	
	Elizabeth	1	"	
Welsh	John	37	72 "	
	Ann	41	"	

177

1820 Census   Catholic Congregation of Preston

Surname	Forename(s)	Age	Address	Comm
[Welsh]	Winifred	9	[High St]	
	John	7	"	
	Joseph	5	"	
	Thomas	4	"	
	Ann	1	"	
Wick	Mary		"	56
Walker	Fanny	57	22 "	
Woods	Thomas	35	29 "	
	Betty	33	"	
	Sally	11	"	
	Ellen	9	"	
	Lucy	7	"	
	William	5	"	
	John	2	"	
	William	33	"	
Whittle	Robert	70	Whittakers Row	
	Peter	32	"	
	Betty	77	"	
Whaley	Ann	74	4 Buxtons Yard	
	Thomas	28	"	
Walmsley	Ralph	28	Bishops passage	
	Betty	3	"	
	Nancy	1	"	
Wareing	Eliza	88	4 Filde St	
Warburton	Henry	33	10 "	
	Ellen	25	"	
	Mary	6	"	
	John	4	"	
	William	2	"	
Woods	John	27	14 Bk Kirkham	
	Ann	26	"	
	William	6	"	
	Mary	3	"	
Waterhouse	John	51	3 Kirkham St	
	Ann	43	"	
	Thomas	19	"	
	Catherine	14	"	
	William	10	"	
	Ann	8	"	
	Joseph	5	"	
	Mary	2	"	
Westry	Thomas	25	1 Snow hill	
	Mary	23	"	
	Jane	2	"	
	James	2	"	
	Catherine	1	"	
Westry	Elizabeth	46	6 "	
	Eliza	19	"	
	Mary	17	"	
	Jane	12	"	

1820 Census — Catholic Congregation of Preston

Surname	Forename(s)	Age	Address	Comm
Wilcock	William	18	34 [Snow hill]	
Walton	Richard	40	10 Vicar	
	Agnes	42	"	
	Mary	17	"	
	Betty	12	"	
	Dorothy	10	"	
	Peter	8	"	
	Thomas	6	"	
	Esabella	4	"	
	Agnes	2	"	
	Richard	1	"	
Wilcock	William	43	12 "	
	Mary	35	"	
	John	11	"	
	Edward	10	"	
	Ann	9	"	
	Elizabeth	5	"	
	Henry	2	"	
Wadiker	William	30	4 Walker	
	Mary	26	"	
Waterhouse	Charles	43	19 Walker Street	
	Margt	30	"	
	William	5	"	
	Helen	3	"	
Waterhouse	James	54	"	
Walmsley	Alice	42	19 "	
	Mary	11	"	
	Joseph	5	"	
	John	4	"	
	Betty		"	
Wilding	William	38	27 "	
	Thomasin	34	"	
	James	10	"	
	Bridget	8	"	
	Richard	6	"	
	John	4	"	
	Ann	1	"	
Worthington	Wm	51	Ribbleton	
	Ann	50	"	
	William	26	"	
	Edward	19		
	Joseph	12	"	
	Mary	7	"	
Whittle	Thomas	53	"	
	Mary	60	"	
	Helen	30	"	
	John	24	"	
	Thomas	20	"	
	Mary	17	"	
Wilkinson	Mary	21	"	

1820 Census   Catholic Congregation of Preston

Surname	Forename(s)	Age	Address	Comm
Worthington	Thomas	24	[Ribbleton]	
	Bridget	31		
	Ann	2	"	
	Lucy	1	"	
Whittle	William	22	"	
	Jane	19	"	
	Mary	1	"	
Wilcock	Thomas	32	Ashton Brows	
	Peggy	47	"	
Wilcock	Ellen	56	Long Lane Ashton	
	George	29	"	
	Ann	21	"	
	John	16	"	
	James	14	"	
Worswick	Rd	22	Nr Tulketh hall	
Wilding	James	26	Long Lane	
	Mary	25	"	
	Betty	3	"	
	Bella	1	"	
Worden	Peter		Fulwood	
	Peggy		"	
Woods	Ellen		"	
Willis	James		"	
Worden	Peter		"	
	Ellen		"	
	James		"	
	William		"	
	Mary		"	
	Ellen		"	
	Thomas		"	
	Peter		"	
Whalley	Ann	74	St John St	
	Thomas	28	"	
Yates	Betty	51	7 St John St	
Yles	Thomas	32	22 Heatley	
	Mary	25	"	
	Richard	6	"	
	Tare? [Tane/Jane?]	1	"	
Young	Margeret		Vauxhall road	
Yates	Mary	14	12 King	
Yates	James	43	Ribbleton	
	Catherine	15	"	
	William	14	"	
	Mary	13	"	
	Mark	11	"	
	James	8	"	
	Thomas	5	"	

1820   A

Atkinson	Thomas	30	Park	
	Ann	30	"	
	Richard	7	"	
	William	4	"	
	Ellen	1	"	
Atkinson	Thomas	15	Nile St	22
Atkinson	Alice	66	Fishergate	28
	James	28	"	
Anderson	Nancy		"	46
	William	17	"	
Arrowsmith	Mary	20	"	53
Branston	Sarah		West end	
Anderson	Richard	16	Mount	32
	Richard	11	"	
Ashurst	Robert	22	Chapel	2
Appleton	Joseph	45	Fishergate	113
	Ellen	48	"	
	Thomas	20	"	
	Ann	19	"	
	Catherine	17	"	
	James	13	"	
	Clare	11	"	
	Margaret	9	"	
	Elizabeth	8	"	
Atkinson	Richard	29	Ratcliff	16
	Alice	24	"	

Example of 1820 entries

Year	No	Comments
1810	1	"Sv to Esqr Dalton"
	2	Friargate substituted for Do
	3	9m substituted for 3/4
	4	"Their Mother a Protestant"
	5	"Has 3 children"
	6	18m substituted for 1 1/2
	7	See Thomas & Mary Walton
	8	Ribbleton Lane substituted for Do
	9	"Miss Mawdesley"
	10	Actual age given is 3 1/2
	11	"Soldier"
	12	"At Mrs Dixons"
	13	"P Catteralls"
	14	"and her 2 brothers"
	15	6m substituted for 1/2
	16	"Sv to Miss Bryers"
	17	Age appears altered from 15 to 17
	18	The 1 of age 15 appears crossed out
	19	"LW' written between age & address
	20	"Sv to Miss Keary"
	21	Age altered from 7
	22	Church St substituted for Do
	23	John St substituted for Do
	24	3m substituted for 1/4
	25	"Has 4 children"
	26	"old man"
	27	"Clerk Catholic Chapel" written in a different hand. To which person does this remark refer?
	28	"Daur of Walsh"
	29	18m substituted for 1 1/2
	30	"Son of the daughter"
	31	"TWNS"
	32	"assist. & niece"

Year	No	Comments
1820	33	"Parents Protestants"
	34	Name may be Martha
	35	Age has been altered, may be 47
	36	"Husband left her"
	37	"This family ought to be called upon"
	38	Church substituted for Do
	39	Surname may be Hunt
	40	"Up yard Nr No 50"
	41	"(at J Holdens)"
	42	"at Newshams"
	43	"servant at J U Wilkinson"
	44	Age not clear, obscured by a blot
	45	"kester" written above Lancaster
	46	Age altered, possibly from 12
	47	Age altered from 51
	48	"North Road at Prestons" added
	49	See Joseph Leach
	50	See Joseph Coupe
	51	"Protestant"
	52	"Market Place" crossed out
	53	House no. not clear, 3 or 36
	54	"Gentlemen wanted here"
	55	"lives at Mellings Vicar St"
	56	"(at Prestons)"

Explanatory Comments

Adamson's Court, Old Shambles
Ainsworth's yard, Church street
Anchor wiend, Market place
Ann street, New Preston
Avenham lane, Syke hill
Avenham road, Avenham lane
Avenham street, Church street
Back Canal street, Friargate
Back Charlotte street, King street
Back Fylde street, Fylde road
Back Kirkham street, Fylde road
Back lane, Lord street
Back Walton street, Leeming street
Back Cotton court, Church street
Bengal place, Dale street
Bishop's Gate, Tythe Barn street
Bishop's Passage, Tythe Barn street
Bleasdale street, Bridge lane
Blue Bell yard, Church street
Bolton's court, Church street
Bolton street, Kirkham street
Boothman's buildings, Marsh lane
Bostock street, Bolton's court
Bow lane, Fishergate
Bowling green, Friargate
Bowman street, Heatley street
Bread street, New Preston
Bridge lane, Bridge street
Bridge street, Friargate
Butler street, Fishergate
Butler's court, Fishergate
Calvert street, King street
Canal street, Friargate
Cannon street, Fishergate
Chandler street, Heatley street
Chapel street, Fishergate
Chapel walks, Fishergate
Charles street, Fishergate
Charlotte street, King street
Cheapside, Market place
Cheetham street, Lord street
Church street (Blackburn &
    Chorley road,) top of Fishergate
Church yard, Church street
Clark yard, Church street

Clayton's yard, Friargate
Cold Bath street, Kirkham street
Cotton court, Church street
Crane's court, Market place
Crown street, Singleton's row
Dale street, Church street
Derby street, Church street
Dover street, near High street
Duke street, King street
Elizabeth street, New Preston
Everton Gardens, St John street
Feeble street, near the Vicarage
Fishergate (Liverpool road) Church st
Fishwick yard, Friargate
Fleet street, Lune street
Foster square, Canal street
Fox street, Fishergate
Frederick street, New Preston
Frenchwood factory, King street
Friargate (Lancaster & Fylde road)
    Market place
Fylde road, Friargate
Fylde street, Fylde road
Ginbow entry, Market place
Glover's court, Fishergate
Graystock's yard, Church street
Great Shawe street, Back lane
Green street, New Preston
Green's yard, Fishergate
Grimshaw street, Church street
Hardman's court, Friargate
Harrison's Hill, Moor lane
Heatley street, Friargate
High street, Tythe Barn street
Hill place, Fishergate
Hope street, Friargate
Horrock's yard, Church street
Houlding's square, Church street
Houlding's yard, Church street
John street, New Preston
Jordan street, Fishergate
King street, Leeming street
Kirkham street, Fylde road
Latus yard, Friargate
Leeming street, Water street

List of Preston Streets in 1821

Library street, St John's place
Lill's yard, Friargate
Lord street, St John street
Lune street, Friargate
Maudlands lane, Fylde road
Market place, top of Friargate,
    Fishergate & Church street
Marsh lane, Fylde road
Minsprit wiend, Church street
Molineux square, Lord street
Moor lane, Friargate
Moor side, Church street
Moss street, Fylde road
Mount pleasant, Chapel street
Mount pleasant, Bridge street
Mount street, Fishergate
New cock yard, Fishergate
New-hall lane, Stanley street
New Preston, New-hall lane
New street, Market place
Nile street, Church street
North street, Patten street
North road, leading
    out of Church street
Old cock yard, Church street
Old Friary, Bridge street
Old Shambles, Market place
Paradise street, King street
Park's court, Fishergate
Patten street, Great Shawe street
Pearson's buildings, Back lane
Peter street, New Preston
Pink street, Rose street
Pitt street, Fishergate
Plantation, Bridge street
Plant's court, Friargate
Pleasant street, Avenham lane
Plough yard, Friargate
Princess street, King street
Ratcliffe street, Heatley street
Ribblesdale place, Chapel street
Ribbleton lane, Church street
Rose street, St John's place
Shambles, Church street & Market place
Shepherd street, Water street
Sill's court, Church street

Simpson street, Heatley street
Singleton's row, Moor lane
Smithson's yard, Market place
Snow hill, Back lane
Spittals moss, Fylde road
Spring gardens, Nile street
Spring street, near Bridge street
Stanley street, Church street
Starch houses, Back lane
St John's place, Church street
St John's street, Church street
Stonygate, St John's place
Strait shambles, Market place
Swainson's court, Cheapside
Swainson's yard, Market place
Syke, Stonygate
Syke hill, Turk's head court
Talbot street, Heatley street
Taylor's court, Friargate
Theatre street, Fishergate
Thomas street, New Preston
Trinity place, Back lane
Turk's head court, Church street
Tythe barn street, Lord street
Union street, Friargate
Vauxhall road, Syke
Vicar street, Snow hill
Vicarage, Bishopgate street
Walker street, Friargate
Walton road, Stanley street
Walton street, Paradise street
Water-lane-end, Marsh lane
Water street, Church street
Water street west, Fishergate
Well street, Heatley street
Wellington street, Crown street
Whittaker's row, St John street
William street, Leeming street
Willow street, Leeming street
Winckley street, Fishergate
Winckley place, Winckley street
Wood street, Lord street
Woodcock's passage, Church street
Woodcock's yard, Fishergate
Woodcock's court, Woodcock's yard
York street, Queen street

List of Preston Streets in 1821